Poetry

  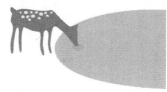

Yorkshire & Lincolnshire

Edited by
Mark Richardson

This book belongs to

First published in Great Britain in 2010 by

 Young**Writers**

Remus House
Coltsfoot Drive
Peterborough
PE2 9JX
Telephone: 01733 890066
Website: www.youngwriters.co.uk

Foreword

At Young Writers our defining aim is to promote an enjoyment of reading and writing amongst children and young adults. By giving aspiring poets the opportunity to see their work in print, their love of the written word as well as confidence in their own abilities has the chance to blossom.

Our latest competition *Poetry Express* was designed to introduce primary school children to the wonders of creative expression. They were given free reign to write on any theme and in any style, thus encouraging them to use and explore a variety of different poetic forms.

We are proud to present the resulting collection of regional anthologies which are an excellent showcase of young writing talent. With such a diverse range of entries received, the selection process was difficult yet very rewarding.

From comical rhymes to poignant verses, there is plenty to entertain and inspire within these pages. We hope you agree that this collection bursting with imagination is one to treasure.

Contents

Wheldrake with Thorganby CE (A) School, Wheldrake

The Poems

Cat In The Window

'Cat in the window,
What do you hear?'

'I can hear birds crunching their food,
I can hear rocks crushing,
I can smell the sea,
With a lot of seaweed,
I can hear a boat,
Leaving behind a big boat.'

Corey Page (10)

My Dad

Hard worker
Clever thinker
Homework helper
Coffee drinker
Home-time lover
Injury recoverer
Art drawer
Working soldier
Music player
Lots of layers
Car driver
Great diver.

Lavua Lord (10)
Alanbrooke Primary School, Thirsk

The Sweet Shop

March down to the sweet shop,
Where all your dreams will come true,
If you want a Yorkie bar or 'you're in the mood' crisps,
Then come down to the sweetie shop
And try some lollipops.

If you are hungry and need to eat sweets,
Then come on down to the sweet shop,
Dime bars with crunchy caramel in the middle,
Crunchy nuts, sugar and sweets,
Come to the sweetie shop and eat, eat, eat!

Marshmallows are mountains of sugar,
Don't eat too many or you might be sick!
We have fairy cakes or pasta bakes.
So come, stroll down to the sweet shop.

Charlotte Daniels (9)
Digby CE School, Digby

Space Sweets

A Galaxy of chocolate,
A Milky Way of sweets,
Gobstoppers as hard as meteors,
A Universe of treats!

We're seeing Mars bar planets
And sherbet saucers flying by,
With little alien Gummy Bears
Waving and saying, 'Hi!'

We're coming back home now,
With fizz pop for fuel,
'Oh no!' Look where we've landed,
In the middle of our school!

Ian Mitchell (11) & Tom Grech (10)
Digby CE School, Digby

Bed In Summer

In winter I get up at night,
And dress up in candlelight.
In summer, quite the other way,
I have to go to bed by day.

I have to go to bed and see
The birds still hopping on the tree,
Or hear the grown-up people's feet,
Still going past me in the street.

And does it not seem hard to you,
When all the sky is clear and blue,
And I would like so much to play,
To have to go to bed by day?

Chloe Shaw (11)
Digby CE School, Digby

That Night

When I went home that night,
a weird little hand turned out the light.
It crawled up my back
and I was sure it was a vampire bat.
Then it crawled on my bed and my scalp bled.
So when I went to my bed, I hid under the covers,
what I found was a hand in my bed.
It weirdly crept over my leg
and quickly snuggled in,
and another hand had a bottle of gin!

Laurence Bonnor (9)
Digby CE School, Digby

The Freaky Door

There is a door that freaks me out,
It scares me, so I scream and shout,
It is so annoying like a bee,
It sits at night and watches me,
I start to scream as the handle turns,
Slowly creaking like a worm,
It starts to open as I hum . . .
But all it is, is my wacky mum!

Rebecca Holt & Lauren Eccles (10)
Digby CE School, Digby

Iron Man

He loves to eat iron but
He does not eat meat,
He didn't have any friends
But he has Hogarth now,
He lives underwater
But not in the clouds,
He has fingers like a bed
But not like a clown,
His head is shaped like a dustbin
But not like a rock,
His body is like a brick but
It is not like sick.

Gavi Mairi Purvis (8)
Fens Primary School, Hartlepool

The Iron Giant

I is for incredibly huge,
R is for his huge, rusty body,
O is for the old metal he eats,
N is for the nice giant he really is.

G is for the gentle giant he is inside,
I is for the intelligence the giant has,
A is for the anger of the farmers,
N is for the number of places he's been,
T is for the tender loving giant that Hogarth sees in him.

Nicole Saffron Davies (9)
Fens Primary School, Hartlepool

Iron Man

I is for Iron Man,
R is for rusty metal,
O is for old metal,
N is for nice,

M is for metal,
A is for arm like a crane,
N is for nobody liked him.

Dean Nicolas Longstaff (8)
Fens Primary School, Hartlepool

The Iron Man

There once was an iron man called Steve
The farmers buried him and said, 'Let's leave
If you give him a car
He won't go that far
He'll stay here and eat all
Who are naïve.'

Scott Skilbeck (8)
Fens Primary School, Hartlepool

Iron Man

I is for iron,
R is for rusty,
O is for all on his own,
N is for no one, he feels all alone.

M is for meat which he cannot eat,
A is for angry when he was trapped in a hole,
N is for he thought no one liked him, he felt he was all on his own.

Benjamin Harry Hart (8)
Fens Primary School, Hartlepool

Iron Man

I is for Iron Man, big and strong,
R is for rusty old metal really long,
O is for on his own a lot,
N is for nearly like a robot.

M is for mainly on his own,
A is for and, he doesn't have a single bone,
N is for now Hogarth is his friend!

Victoria Cranney (8)
Fens Primary School, Hartlepool

The Iron Man

I n the open world hunting for scrap,
R unning up and down the scrapyard,
O n the land marching around,
N aughty scavenger hunting for food.

M etal eater always hungry,
A giant monster on the loose,
N o one knows where he came from.

Joseph Henry Tyers (9)
Fens Primary School, Hartlepool

Iron Man

I s very greedy and loves to eat,
R ed headlamps that shine in the dark,
O ld rusty tractors and metal in the fields,
N obody would ever want to be his friend except from Hogarth.

M iles and miles they go trying to find the monster,
A lways wanting more than one friend,
N ever wanting to see the monster again.

Libby Serginson (8)
Fens Primary School, Hartlepool

The Iron Man

I n their heads, he is a monster.
R ats running around getting squished.
O n the run, eating metal.
N o one knows what he is like.

M onster eating metal tractors.
A hill getting cracked.
N ow he has got a friend.

Anthony Stokle (9)
Fens Primary School, Hartlepool

Iron Man

There was once an iron man called Ste,
Who liked to admire the sea,
He then fell down,
It made him frown,
And what a silly man was he!

Louis Marchant (8)
Fens Primary School, Hartlepool

Lion

They are as fast as a hare.
They are mad like Mr Bentham.
They are as fierce as a crocodile.
They are hungry like a wave.
They are as nasty as a rhino.
They are as fat as a hippo.
They are cruel like a cheetah.
They are as grumpy as an old man.
They are furry like a monkey.
It is a lion.

Riley Bowen-Lagden (7)
Fortuna Primary Special School, Lincoln

Brother

He is as soft as a sofa.
He is as cute as a pet.
He is as clever as a scientist.
He is as lazy as a teddy.
He is as brainy as a professor.
He is as friendly as a robot.
He is as kind as a friend.
He is as gentle as a star.
He is as cuddly as a bear.
He is my brother.

Kristian Hughes (9)
Fortuna Primary Special School, Lincoln

Diamond

It is as mighty as a bull
It is as shiny as glass
It is as glamorous as my mum
It is as magnificent as a whale
It is as powerful as an elephant
It is as gorgeous as a flower
It is as astonishing as my mum
It is as indestructible as the sun
It is a diamond.

Kyle Dilley (10)
Fortuna Primary Special School, Lincoln

Lion

It is as angry as a cook
It is as orange as a motorbike
It is as dangerous as Mr Bentham
It is as fast as a car
It is as nasty as a crocodile
It is as miserable as a windy day
It is as scary as a ghost
It is as fierce as the sun
It is a lion.

Connor Johnson (8)
Fortuna Primary Special School, Lincoln

Mum

She is as peaceful as a lake.
She is as fascinating as a diamond.
She is as beautiful as a star.
She is as scared as a spider.
She is as cross as a volcano.
She is as happy as a cat.
She is my mum.

James Cook (8)
Fortuna Primary Special School, Lincoln

Power Rangers

They are as tough as an eagle.
They are as powerful as robots.
They are as cool as a cool dude.
They are as red as the sun.
They are as helpful as a good guy.
They are as brave as a tiger.
They are Power Rangers.

Marcus-Blayne Hepworth (7)
Fortuna Primary Special School, Lincoln

Volcano

V icious volcano
O ut in the air
L ava everywhere
C rumbly rocks in the air
A mber lava spits out fire
N oisy rock flies out the top
O utstanding volcano.

Charlotte Hitchen (7)
Fountains CE Primary School, Ripon

Under The Sea

U nder the rocks crabs creep like mice.
N o fish are as fierce as a shark.
D olphins dive deep.
E els slither around.
R ay fish race.

T urtles turn round and round.
H undreds of fish swim by.
E lephant seals swim happily.

S tingrays sting.
E vil swordfish swim.
A nemones stick to rocks.

Cameron Knox (8)
Fountains CE Primary School, Ripon

Under The Sea

U nder the sea
N utty newt
D ancing dogfish
E lectric eels
R usty ray

T remendous tuna
H yper hammerhead shark
E xotic elephant seal

S harks swim as they find food
E els move side to side like a crab
A ncient anemone.

Belinda Hosie (8)
Fountains CE Primary School, Ripon

Deep Down In The Ocean Wide

U nder the sea is lots of glee
N asty newts are very cute
D iving dolphins dip in the sea
E llie the eel lives in orange peel
R ock fish fib

T illy the tuna
H atching haddock hunt for heat
E lectric eels look for meals

S tingrays sting like we enjoy spring
E lliott the echoing fish
A lice the alligator.

Tilly Wills (8)
Fountains CE Primary School, Ripon

Different Fish

U nder the sea
N asty newt
D izzy dolphin
E els move side to side like a crab
R usty rowing boat

T errific tuna
H ungry haddock
E xcited jellyfish jump like kangaroos

S tinging stingray
E vil shark swims by
A ngry alligator.

Rebecca Grange (9)
Fountains CE Primary School, Ripon

Under The Sea

U gly catfish swims by as
N aughty as a shark
D olphins diving everywhere
E lectric eels don't power light
R eally they just give you a fright

T urtles paddling by
H airy urchin eats its prey
E xhausted whale just learnt to swim

S haggy shark
E normous blue whale
A mmonite is so spirally.

Oscar Taylor (9)
Fountains CE Primary School, Ripon

In The Deep, Deep Sea

U gly catfish swimming by
N atural
D evil dog up above
E normous whale eats some grub
R eally squirmy squid

T he pufferfish can pop a balloon
H aul of trout
E xtraordinary shark

S alty water stings your eyes
E llie's electric eel swimming by
A group of turtles plodding past.

Michael Sorby (8)
Fountains CE Primary School, Ripon

Under The Sea

U gly catfish swimming by.
N urse shark swimming speedily.
D iver is splashing in the sea.
E lectric eel electrocuting people.
R ay fish is relaxing in the sea water.

T urtle is slowly moving in the sea.
H ow I wish I was a fish.
E ating oysters all day long.

S tarfish sparkling in the waves.
E lephant seal killing penguins.
A mazing alligators.

Benjamin Thomas (8)
Fountains CE Primary School, Ripon

Under The Sea

U nder the rocks crabs creep like mice.
N othing is as nice as a newt.
D ancing like a ballerina, dolphins dance the dazzling seas.
E lectric eels strike like snakes.
R ough rays glide along.

T he terrific sound of a whale's song.
H ear it as you go along.
E nemies as nasty as a great white shark.

S ea anemones swaying like tree branches.
E erie sounds as noisy as a blasting rocket taking off!
A methysts lie there, under the sea.

Eloise Spick (8)
Fountains CE Primary School, Ripon

Deep Down

U gly fish eating
N asty sharks eat
D aring divers go deep down
E lephant fish
R usty rattle shark

T ingling tiger shark
H atchet fish
E els eating away

S hivering sea snake
E xcited X-ray fish
A ngry anglerfish.

Hallam Brammah (8)
Fountains CE Primary School, Ripon

My Bedroom

M arvellous toys,
Y ellow walls like bananas,

B ouncy bed,
E verlasting excitement,
D inosaur posters everywhere,
R acing cars race around their track,
O rnaments shaking on my wardrobe,
O ut come my toys,
M aking mess every day for my mum to clean up.

Joshua Pillar (8)
Fountains CE Primary School, Ripon

Fish

F ish under the deep blue sea.
I sland is a nice place, can you see?
S ometimes it's raining, dark and dim.
H opping jellyfish swimming deeply in the sea.

Sophie Andrew (7)
Fountains CE Primary School, Ripon

Titanic

Olympic sister
Ice breaker
Smoke maker
Crew killer
Panic maker
Money taker
Lifeboat carrier
Rivet failure
3rd class losers
New life maker
Metal breaker
Time taker
Star Line leader
Midnight faller
1st class butler
Water shaker
California rescuer
New York intender
Life snatcher
Cruise liner.

Katrina Hostad (8)
Goxhill Primary School, Goxhill

Titanic

22-knot speed maker,
Boat breaker,
Panic maker,
Star Line maker,
Money taker,
Rivet failer,
Olympic sister,
Cruise liner,
1st class butler,
Metal breaker,
Risk taker,
Southampton starter,
New life seeker,
Ice breaker,
Life taker,
Nit checker,
1st class dreamer,
Steam maker,
Ocean floater,
Worst ship ever!

Neve Ruddick (8)
Goxhill Primary School, Goxhill

Shark - Haiku

They are quite deadly
Their tails can swish all around
Sharp, pointy teeth chew.

Adam Carn (9)
Goxhill Primary School, Goxhill

Titanic

Ice breaker,
Boat sinker,
Big sinker,
Cruise liner,
Water glider,
New York leader,
Southampton starter,
New life seeker,
1st class dreamer,
Ocean leader,
Gigantic disaster,
Money taker,
Olympic sister,
Nit checker,
3rd class loser,
Time nicer,
Risk taker,
Metal glider,
Midnight cruiser,
Coffin taker.

Jack Clapson (7)
Goxhill Primary School, Goxhill

Haiku

As cheeky as me
As fast as a huge cheetah
Big, cheeky, blue eyes.

Ben Whall (9)
Goxhill Primary School, Goxhill

Titanic

Iceberg breaker
Cruise liner
New life seeker
Steam maker
Time chaser
Nit checker
1st class dreamer
White Star Line owner
Rivet failer
Olympic sister
New York chaser
Gigantic disaster
22-knot speed maker
Iceberg warning ignorer
Risk taker
Midnight sinker
Life taker.

Abigail Anderson (7)
Goxhill Primary School, Goxhill

Titanic

Cruise liner,
People kinder,
Dining room lighter,
Swift swimmer,
New life seeker,
Midnight sinker,
California annoyer,
Tragedy maker,
Iceberg fighter
Panic causer.

India Wilson (7)
Goxhill Primary School, Goxhill

Titanic

Holiday maker,
Trembling shaker,
New life spender,
Iceberg crasher,
Gigantic disaster,
3rd class loser,
3rd class boozer,
Holiday snoozer,
1st class dreamer,
Holiday seeker,
Marconi talker,
Very hot boiler,
Boat sinker,
I am . . .
Titanic!

Mollie Kerby (7)
Goxhill Primary School, Goxhill

Titanic

Cruise liner,
Iceberg fighter,
Ice chipper,
Unsinkable figure,
Tragedy maker,
Midnight sinker,
Panic causer,
Lifeboat loser,
Midnight cruiser,
Big bruiser,
Huge diner,
Expensive liner.

Charlotte Cawkwell (7)
Goxhill Primary School, Goxhill

Animal · Haiku

Canters and gallops
Jumps as high as the houses
Eats carrots and hay.

Leah Scott (9)
Goxhill Primary School, Goxhill

Animal · Haiku

Eats a lot of food
As spotty as a cheetah
Lives in a forest.

Lucie Mosey (8)
Goxhill Primary School, Goxhill

Animal · Haiku

Sly, creepy movement
They have orange, bushy tails.
Silent as a mouse.

Georgia Hynes (9)
Goxhill Primary School, Goxhill

Animal · Haiku

They are real rascals
They run and pounce every day
They're cute and cuddly.

Eliot Tucker (9)
Goxhill Primary School, Goxhill

Animal · Haiku

A tall animal.
An energetic, smart pet.
A great pet to have.

Zoe Newton (9)
Goxhill Primary School, Goxhill

Animal · Haiku

Snow falls from the sky
Get inside your warm, soft bed
The plants are all gone.

Casey Dommett (8)
Goxhill Primary School, Goxhill

Animal · Haiku

Walking quietly.
Prowling in the boiling sun.
Creeping up on mice.

Molly Lus (8)
Goxhill Primary School, Goxhill

Animal · Haiku

As small as a frog.
Patters around the fields fast.
Cute, soft, furry ears.

Megan Russell (9)
Goxhill Primary School, Goxhill

Animal - Haiku

As slow as syrup.
Astonishing as apples.
As bold as a stone.

Alex Dawson (8)
Goxhill Primary School, Goxhill

Animal - Haiku

Big, tired, fat feet
Move as slowly as a snail,
Cooling down in mud!

Amelia Wilson (8)
Goxhill Primary School, Goxhill

Animal - Haiku

Fluffy, cuddly, soft.
Chasing cats round the garden.
Cute as a bunny.

Neive Atkin (9)
Goxhill Primary School, Goxhill

Fab Style

F unky hat
A symmetrical dress
B racelet that sparkles

S hiny shoes
T rendy tops
Y ummy clothes
L ifelong beauty
E ngraved make-up.

Nicole Bruce (11)
Haxby Road Primary School, York

Danielle Martin

D anielle dances round her room
A nd loves to sing to Leona Lewis
N ever ever gives up
I am quite good at maths
E veryone likes her
L oves her mum and her family
L oves her boyfriend
E veryone likes her best friend

M egan's her best friend
A lways shops with her best friend
R hiannon, her friend, is really weird
T otally cool
I s obese with big chins
N obody knows what world she lives in.

Danielle Martin (11)
Haxby Road Primary School, York

Call Of Duty

C O D
A fghan
L ethal weapons
L ots of kills

O utstanding glitches
F avela

D ragnov
U mp45
T hompson
Y oung killers.

Aaran Wrigglesworth (11)
Haxby Road Primary School, York

Shopaholic

S hopping
H andbags
O ffers and sales
P urses
A ll different sizes
H air bands
O r clips
L ipstick
I need them all, especially more
C lothes!

Megan Flanagan (10)
Haxby Road Primary School, York

Man United

M anchester, champions of England.
A mazing Rooney scores again.
N ew players for the champs, an unbeatable team.

U nited forever.
N eed to win the title again.
I mpresses everyone.
T eamwork of the highest quality.
E ncourages every child to play football.
D emanding everyone, they play.

Ryan Kettlestring (10)
Haxby Road Primary School, York

Mr Sandman

Mr Sandman, sprinkle your dust,
I'm waiting for something, nothing that much,
Just one little dream,
Something good,
I would do anything, anything I would,
If I could give you the world,
Believe me I would,
Mr Sandman give me a dream.

Allison Hewitt (11)
Haxby Road Primary School, York

Arsenal

A rsenal scoring goals faster than lightning
R apid Arshavin running down the pitch
S ong being a great defender
E mirates is where they play
N othing can get in their way
A rsene Wenger is their manager
L ots of goals they score, whenever they play.

Sajjad Hussein (10)
Haxby Road Primary School, York

Teacher

T he teacher's always being bossy.
E ats lots of biscuits and drinks coffee.
A lways giving us homework.
C hanging the subject.
H omework for us again.
E ats more biscuits.
R eally, do I have to put up with this?

Holly Markwick (10)
Haxby Road Primary School, York

Foster, My Cat

F urry and friendly cat
O bviously cute and cuddly
S leeps all day, eats all night
T earing my blanket
E veryone loves him
R eturns every night.

Rhiannon Cochrane (10)
Haxby Road Primary School, York

Fish

F ins swish in the water.
I n the seas they swim.
S hort tails sway.
H ate those sharks!

Jessica Green (10)
Haxby Road Primary School, York

The Tiger

I am stripy as a zebra.
I am so fast and smooth.
I am as scary as a monster.
I have teeth as pointy as knives.

I have bright red eyes like a fire.
I have short, light brown ears.
I live in a spooky forest.
I have some claws as pointy as nails.

Sophie Long (7)
Hob Moor Community Primary School, Acomb

The Mysterious Candle

The flame is a . . .

Golden diamond
Twinkling on a burning wick
Shining coin
Dropped from a golden drain in Heaven
Gift from God
Blazing in the night
Pretty skater
Dancing on the wax
Calm, peaceful sunset
Glowing in the dreamy summer sky

The wax is . . .

Fiery volcano
Dribbling along the lumpy rocks
Glistening river of lava
Flowing down the candle
Young girl
Weeping silently as each tear slides down
Soft, crystal-clear waterfall
Flowing down the mountainside
Gorgeous fountain

The smoke is . . .

Stealthy ghost
Creeping away into the midnight darkness
Wandering cloud
Travelling until it is seen no more
Floating ghost
Wandering through the ghostly graveyard

Shivering cold ghost
Freezing in the night
Whispering secret
So silent and calm.

Amelia Hall (10)
Hob Moor Community Primary School, Acomb

The Candle

The flame is a . . .
Dancing angel
Prancing as it burnishes and flickers,
A shimmering butterfly
Fluttering through the dark night,
Showing light wherever it goes,
A joyful star
Giving light to all the world.

The wax is a . . .
Calm river
Flowing down the side of a cliff,
Almost a waterfall
Silent and graceful,
Erupting volcano
With fiery lava dripping down the cool dry rock,
A crystal-clear teardrop
Dripping down the cheek of a lonely girl.

The smoke is a . . .
Ghostly shadow
Whispering mysteriously as it disappears into the dark,
A black cloud
Hovering over the city,
A ghostly hand
Waving around, almost invisible
And hiding away where no one can see.

Lauren Calvert (10)
Hob Moor Community Primary School, Acomb

Candle

The flame is . . .
A glimmering diamond
Flashing in the lightless unknown,
A shining warrior
Fighting off the darkness,
A fiery butterfly
Fluttering in the cool midnight air,
A beautiful sunset
Giving brightness to the world.

The wax is . . .
A golden fish
Swimming down the murky river,
A blazing wave
Shooting down the mountainside,
A mysterious sea
Flowing down the secret mountain,
A giant tear
Dripping peacefully down to Earth.

The smoke is . . .
A broken-hearted ghost
Screeching in the darkness,
A coiling snake
Drifting up to Heaven above,
A cryptic shadow
Wandering slowly, disappearing into the unknown,
A swirling cloud
Floating above the burning city.

Zach Brown (10)
Hob Moor Community Primary School, Acomb

The Candle

The flame is a . . .
Bright angel
Flying like a bird up to Heaven,
Golden ghost
Disappearing without a trace,
Twinkling star
Shining like a diamond in the dark night.

The wax is a . . .
Scalding river
Burning down the steep edge,
Volcano's lava
Running down the edge of a cliff,
Runny liquid
Running away from the tap.

The smoke is a . . .
Whispering moth
Fluttering silently through the dark night,
Slithering snake
Floating away, leaving no trace,
A grey ghost
Disappearing into thin air.

Thomas Power (11)
Hob Moor Community Primary School, Acomb

The Sun

The cloud
Opened its mouth and . . .
Smiled and . . .
The sun popped out.
Like a spider with glowing arms,
It dangled from the sky.

Kerrianne Moynes (11)
Hornsea Community Primary School, Hornsea

31

The Seaside

The seagulls gather around the fishing boats,
in the harbour they all fly.
They swoop and dive for our tray of chips,
and they sometimes make me cry.

But that won't stop us coming,
to see the changing tide.
We love our days together,
when we go to the seaside.

With the waves cascading
onto the golden sandy beach,
we hope that our village of sandcastles,
the water will not reach.

When we paddle in the shimmering sea,
our mother really does fret,
because we like to kick up water at her
and try to get her clothes *wet!*

My brother is very competitive
and always wants to race,
but the other sunbathers don't like it,
when we run past and kick sand in their face.

My sister likes to collect seashells;
her collection is now quite large,
but Dad turns angry when we reach home,
because she stores them in his garage.

We also take a picnic for lunch,
but I will never understand,
it doesn't matter how well you pack it,
your sandwiches are always covered in sand!

When the sun's going down and it's time to go,
we often become really sad.
Dad makes us laugh on the journey home,
remembering the fun day we just had.

So when the sun is shining down on us,
there's nowhere else I'd rather be,
than spending days at the seaside,
with the whole of my family.

Megan Wilson (10)
Hornsea Community Primary School, Hornsea

Tell, Tell, Tell

(Inspired by 'Frying Pan In A Moving Van' by Eve Merriam)

I went to a new school this term.
What did you see?
Tell, tell, tell.

Well I saw a wooden chair with a plastic pear
What else did you see?
Tell, tell, tell.

Well I saw a swimming pool with a man with a tool
And a wooden chair with a plastic pear.
What else did you see?
Tell, tell, tell.

Well I saw a dolly in Mrs Dearing's trolley
And a swimming pool with a man with a tool
And a wooden chair with a plastic pear
What else did you see?
Tell, tell, tell.

Well I saw Mr Walker with a trolley and Mr Kirk with a summer brolly.

What did you see?
Tell, tell, tell.
Well I saw Jordan being Gordon
That's all I saw.

Sam Cowie (11)
Hornsea Community Primary School, Hornsea

My New School

(Inspired by 'Frying Pan In A Moving Van' by Eve Merriam)

I went to a new school this term.
What did you see? Tell, tell, tell.
Well I saw a rubbish bin next to a red pencil tin.

What else did you see? Tell, tell, tell.
Well I saw a boy called Kyle and some books in a pile.
A rubbish bin next to a red pencil tin.

What else did you see? Tell, tell, tell.
Well I saw Mr Walker with a trolley and Mr Kirk with a summer brolly.
A boy called Kyle and books in a pile.
A rubbish bin next to a red pencil tin.

What else did you see? Tell, tell, tell.
Well I saw a Lego bridge and the fruit fridge
Mr Walker with a trolley and Mr Kirk with a summer brolly.
A boy called Kyle and books in a pile.
A rubbish bin next to a red pencil tin.

What else did you see? Tell, tell, tell.
Well I saw Ben Wait but he arrived late
and I saw a Lego bridge and the fruit fridge
and Mr Walker with a trolley and Mr Kirk with a summer brolly
and a boy called Kyle and books in a pile
and a rubbish bin next to a red pencil tin.

What else did you see? Tell, tell, tell.
Well since you ask
I saw Ben Wait, but he arrived late, with a mate
and I saw a Lego bridge, the fruit fridge, and a tool ridge
and Mr Walker with a trolley, Mr Kirk with a summer brolly,

a girl playing with a plastic dolly
and a boy called Kyle and books in a pile and a roof tile
and a rubbish bin next to a red pencil tin
and a child sewing with a pin.

And that's all I saw at my new school this term.

Benjamin Wait (10)
Hornsea Community Primary School, Hornsea

New School

(Inspired by 'Frying Pan In A Moving Van' by Eve Merriam)

I went to a new school this term
What did you see?
Tell, tell, tell.

Well I saw Polly with a lolly in Mrs Dearing's trolley.
What else did you see?
Tell, tell, tell.

I saw a ball in the floor and a big blue door.
Polly with a lolly in Mrs Dearing's trolley.
What else did you see?
Tell, tell, tell.

I saw a keyboard and a golden award.
Polly with a lolly in Mrs Dearing's trolley.
A ball on the floor and a big blue door.
What else did you see?
Tell, tell, tell.

I saw a jelly going in someone's belly and a telly.
A keyboard and a golden award.
Polly with a lolly in Mrs Dearing's trolley.
A ball on the floor and a big blue door.

And that's all I saw at my new school.

Jake Sullivan (10)
Hornsea Community Primary School, Hornsea

A New School

(Inspired by 'Frying Pan In A Moving Van' by Eve Merriam)

I went to a new school this term.
What did you see?
Tell, tell, tell.

Well I saw a broken wall and a basketball.
What else did you see?
Tell, tell, tell.

Well I saw a rubbish bin and a pencil tin,
And a broken wall and a basketball.
What else did you see?
Tell, tell, tell.

Well I saw a wooden table and a bright orange cable,
And a rubbish bin and a pencil tin,
And a broken wall and a basketball.
What else did you see?
Tell, tell, tell.

Well I saw an ice lolly in Mrs Dearing's trolley,
And a wooden table and a bright orange cable,
And a rubbish bin and a pencil tin,
And a broken wall and a basketball.
What else did you see?
Tell, tell, tell.

Well, now you're asking,
I saw an old shed, a wooden bed, and someone with a bumped head
And an ice lolly in Mrs Dearing's trolley and someone with a dolly.
A wooden table and a bright orange cable and a girl called Mabel,
And a broken wall and a basketball, and a boy who was tall,
And a pencil tin and a little pin.

That is what I saw at school today.

Chloe Dann (10)
Hornsea Community Primary School, Hornsea

First Day At School

(Inspired by 'Frying Pan In A Moving Van' by Eve Merriam)

I went to a new school this term
What did you see?
Tell, tell, tell.

Well I saw a broken wall and a basketball.
What else did you see?
Tell, tell, tell.

Well I saw a rubbish bin and a pencil tin,
And a broken wall and a basketball.
What else did you see?
Tell, tell, tell.

Well, I saw a first aid kit and a girl being hit,
A rubbish bin and a pencil tin,
And a broken wall and a basketball.
What else did you see?
Tell, tell, tell.

Well, I saw a fruit trolley with Miss Dolly,
A first aid kit and a girl being hit,
A rubbish bin and a pencil tin,
And a broken wall and a basketball.
What else did you see?
Tell, tell, tell

Well, since you ask, I saw a girl called Chloe, with a girl called Zoe,
Talking to a boy called Joey.
A fruit trolley with Miss Dolly, who always looks so very jolly,
A first aid kit and a girl being hit, a candle being lit,
A rubbish bin and a pencil tin, Olivia trying to make her work fit in,
And a broken wall and a basketball and Mr Bridges looking oh so
tall.

And that is all I saw at my new school this term.

Olivia Codd (10)
Hornsea Community Primary School, Hornsea

My New School

(Inspired by 'Frying Pan In A Moving Van' by Eve Merriam)

I went to a new school this term.
What did you see?
Tell, tell, tell.

Well I saw a messy drawer and a soggy wet floor.
What else did you see?
Tell, tell, tell

Well I saw a broken table and a girl called Mabel,
And a messy drawer and a soggy wet floor.
What else did you see?
Tell, tell, tell.

Well I saw a rubbish bin and a pencil tin,
And a broken table and a girl called Mabel,
And a messy drawer and a soggy wet floor.
What else did you see?
Tell, tell, tell.

Well I saw a fruit trolley and a girl called Molly with her little dolly.
A rubbish bin and a pencil tin and a boy called Finn.
A broken table and a girl called Mabel,
And a messy drawer and a soggy wet floor.
What else did you see?
Tell, tell, tell.

Well since you ask it, I saw a wooden basket,
And a fruit trolley and a girl called Molly with her dolly with a lolly,
And a broken table and a girl called Mabel and a colourful cable,
And a basketball hoop and a bowl full of soup and a girl going
whoop.
And a messy drawer and a soggy wet floor and a wooden door.

And that's all I saw in my new school.

Rebecca Coates (10)
Hornsea Community Primary School, Hornsea

A New School

(Inspired by 'Frying Pan In A Moving Van' by Eve Merriam)

I went to a new school this term.
What did you see?
Tell, tell, tell.
Well I saw a dirty rubbish bin with a pencil tin.
What else did you see?
Tell, tell, tell
Well I saw a man with a door and the carpet on the floor
and a dirty rubbish bin with a pencil tin.
What else did you see?
Tell, tell, tell.
Well I saw a dolly in Mrs Dearing's trolley
and a man with a door and the carpet on the floor
and a dirty rubbish bin and a pencil tin.
What else did you see?
Tell, tell, tell.
Well I saw a man with a ball and the goal down the hall
and a dolly in Mrs Dearing's trolley
and a man with a door and the carpet on the floor
and a dirty rubbish bin and a pencil tin.
What else did you see?
Tell, tell, tell.
Well since you ask it, I saw a man with a rocking chair
and someone saying a prayer and Joe trying to share.
A man with a ball and the goal down the hall.
A man with a baseball bat in the city hall
and a dolly in Mrs Dearing's trolley
and a man with a door and the carpet on the floor
and a mucky whiteboard and a dirty rubbish bin and a pencil tin.

And that's all I saw at my new school.

Richard Westoby (10)
Hornsea Community Primary School, Hornsea

New School
(Inspired by 'Frying Pan In A Moving Van' by Eve Merriam)

I went to a new school this term.
What did you see?
Tell, tell, tell
Well, I saw a fox in a box
And a red peg on a rabbit's leg
And a green paper bin and a black pencil tin.
What else did you see?
Tell, tell, tell

Well, I saw a cat with a bat
And a fox in a box
And a red peg on a rabbit's leg
And a green paper bin and a black pencil tin.
What else did you see?
Tell, tell, tell

Well, I saw a library book and the school cook
And a cat with a bat
And a fox in a box
And a red peg on a rabbit's leg
And a green paper bin and a black pencil tin.
What else did you see?
Tell, tell, tell

Well since you ask
I saw a library book, the school cook and a captain's hook
And a cat with a bat and a big black rat
And a fox in a box and a baby ox
And a red peg on a rabbit's leg and a colourful egg
And a green paper bin, a black pencil tin and a shiny pin.

And that's all I saw at my new school.

Rheace Prescott (11)
Hornsea Community Primary School, Hornsea

The Roller Coaster

The safety bars locked around my head
I was quaking with fear.
Slowly, I began to move
Daylight burst out clear.
Suddenly, to my dismay
The ground began to drop away.
I climbed and climbed very high
I felt that I could touch the sky!

Then I began to fall
Rushing through the air.
I could feel the wind against my face
Brushing through my hair.
All of a sudden, my carriage spun, crushing me into my seat
Grinning to myself, I decided, this ride couldn't be beat!

Then the carriage swooped straight down, into the loop-the-loop
The world span round and round.
It was then I realised why I felt sick . . .
I was travelling upside down!

Slowly the ride stopped
I hurriedly clambered out.
I realised I was going to be sick
I looked to see if there was a bin about.
There was one, I ran towards it
But I didn't make it in time.

My stomach was emptied
My head was in a spin.
But no worries at least
For the clean, sparkling dustbin!

Jack Farmer (11)
Hornsea Community Primary School, Hornsea

I Went To A New School

(Inspired by 'Frying Pan In A Moving Van' by Eve Merriam)

I went to a new school this term.
What did you see?
Tell, tell, tell.
Well I saw a little swimming pool in the big old school
and a broken wall and a basketball
and a dirty rubbish bin and a red pencil tin.
What else did you see?
Tell, tell, tell.
Well I saw a fish in a tank with a boy that looked like a plank
and a little swimming pool in the big old school
and a broken wall and a basketball
and a dirty rubbish bin and a red pencil tin.
What else did you see?
Tell, tell, tell.
I saw a sweeping brush and a toilet flush
and a little swimming pool in the big old school
and a broken wall and a basketball
and a dirty rubbish bin and a red pencil tin.
What else did you see?
Tell, tell, tell
I saw a sweeping brush, a toilet flush and a spiky old bush
and a little swimming pool in the big old school
and a man with a tool.
And a broken wall and a basket ball and a bird's call
and a dirty rubbish bin and a red pencil tin.

And that is all I saw in the new school.

Marcus Ford (11)
Hornsea Community Primary School, Hornsea

New School

(Inspired by 'Frying Pan In A Moving Van' by Eve Merriam)

I went to a new school this term.
What did you see? Tell, tell, tell.
Well I saw a red bin and a blueberry tin.
What else did you see? Tell, tell, tell.
I saw Nathan rapping and Callum lapping and a red bin
and a blueberry tin.
What else did you see? Tell, tell, tell.
I saw a broken wall and a basketball. I saw Nathan rapping
and Callum lapping and a red bin and a blueberry tin.
What else did you see? Tell, tell, tell.
I saw Ben Wait on a date and Declan who was late. A broken wall
and a basketball. I saw Nathan rapping and Callum lapping
and a red bin and a blueberry tin.
What else did you see? Tell, tell, tell.
Well I saw Kyle being a pest and a money chest. Ben Wait on a date
and Declan who was late, a broken wall and a basketball.
I saw Nathan rapping and Callum lapping and a red bin
and a blueberry tin.
What else did you see? Tell, tell, tell.
Well since you ask
I saw Nathan rapping and Callum lapping and Kyle scrapping,
a broken wall and a basketball and a boy who was tall,
Ben Wait on a date, Declan who was late coming through
the school gate. A red bin, a blueberry tin and a match to win.
And that's all I saw at my new school.

Callum Stanley (10)
Hornsea Community Primary School, Hornsea

Chickens!

Four chicks we wanted,
Four chicks we got,
Some grew larger,
And some did not.

Trevor soon learnt to *cock-a-doodle-doo,*
And every morning he woke up Sue,
But still no eggs from the other three,
Bertha, Nugget and little Gertie.

Then one morning with even more noise,
Gertie and Bertha had turned into boys,
Three cocks we were left with and just one hen,
Poor Nugget was left with Bert and Gavin.

So what did we do to prevent all the fights?
We couldn't stay up any more nights,
Bert had to go, the largest of them all,
We gave him to the man next door, his name was Paul.

In return for Bert he gave us a hen,
We named her Tallulah, a Buff Orpington,
For two nights she joined our other three,
They lived together happily.

And then this morning to our surprise,
We found an egg and it was a good size,
Sue, sleepy and tired, was amazed and said, 'Great!'
And then took her revenge and cooked it for her plate.

Emily Horsfall (11)
Hornsea Community Primary School, Hornsea

In the Fruit Bowl

Sitting here,
In a corner,
All alone in the bowl,
No one to talk to,
Tired.

Come closer,
Need a friend,
Need eating.
Neglected, abandoned,
My eyes are shimmering.

Round, perfect,
Like a shining globe,
So juicy,
Waiting with excitement,
As you come closer.

You pick me up,
I'm being eaten,
Gently enveloped,
End of my life,
I loved that experience,
No longer forsaken!

Emily Coates (11)
Hornsea Community Primary School, Hornsea

Bella

Sleeping - waking,
Eating treats.
Living - dying,
Birthday treats.
Happy - sad,
Walking treats.
Sitting - standing,
There you meet.

Bella, my girl, you leap into darkness,
As I watch you I cry,
From the morning sunlight to the moonlight dark sky,
The door gulps you in, while the windows glare at you
With their beady eyes.

Sleeping - waking,
Eating treats.
Living - dying,
Birthday treats.
Happy - sad,
Walking treats.
Sitting - standing,
There you meet.

Saffron Baldwin (10)
Hornsea Community Primary School, Hornsea

The Beach

Watery sunshine,
Blinks through the clouds.
Seaweed waves goodbye.
Children leap, like leopards, across smooth, silky sand.

Rebecca Willis (10)
Hornsea Community Primary School, Hornsea

Puppy Love

There in the window,
a forlorn, upset face,
stares through the trapped cage,
without any space.

Poor and defenceless,
with 'take me home' eyes.
No wagging tail.
Will anyone hear her cries?

If only she could be
a dog with a home.
Being part of a family,
she would never be alone.

Frustrated and angry,
tears cascade down my face.
Passionate and determined,
I'll get her out of this place!

Whipping, wagging tail.
Big, bright eyes are alive.
I pay my money.
Now she's mine!

Imogen Scott (10)
Hornsea Community Primary School, Hornsea

Sun

The sun is a bright, leaping circle of fire,
Twirling in and out of white clouds.
The wind -
A storming blizzard,
Destroying everything with its breath.

Ellie Clappison (11)
Hornsea Community Primary School, Hornsea

Happy Family

Mother, Brother, Sister, laughing and joking,
Dad, Grandad trying to untie a buckle,
Cousin on the Game Station,
Aunty making pots of tea,

A happy atmosphere.

Grandma patiently waiting,
Delicious smells waft through the air,
Makes Great Grandma smack her lips,
With anticipation for her meal,

A happy atmosphere,
A buzzing atmosphere.

Finally sitting down to lunch,
For a wonderful roast meal.
Tender beef, roasted potatoes,
An army of colourful vegetables,
Everyone relaxing and munching.

A happy atmosphere,
A buzzing atmosphere,
I love a happy family!

Amy Balfour (10)
Hornsea Community Primary School, Hornsea

Wintry White

W intry white waves walloping the sand,
E ndless gusts of grey groaning wind,
A ngry, relentless rain rattling on the roof,
T errible torrents flooding through the towns,
H urricanes hammering helpless homes,
E vaporating water vapour enters the empty air,
R ays of shining sunlight slicing through the stormy clouds.

Charlie Rowbotham (11)
Hornsea Community Primary School, Hornsea

King Of The Trees

Branch swinger,
Tree jumper,
Piercing screecher,
Mad laugher,
Nit picker,
Bogey flicker,
Leaf licker,
Peanut sheller,
Nut nibbler,
Flea cruncher,
Termite muncher,
Fruit lover,
Banana peeler,
Tail hanger,
Hair groomer,
Beetle crusher,
Armpit scratcher,
Trouble causer,
Mischief maker,
Monkey performer!

Max Evans (10)
Hornsea Community Primary School, Hornsea

The Old London Train Station

He arrives home,
The platform filthy as a memory,
Chewing gum pocks the floor.
The cracked, shattered gates open for me,
This is where I belong!
Pushed! Shoved! No love!
I shop,
Then back to boring Hornsea.

Maegan Rawdon (10)
Hornsea Community Primary School, Hornsea

Vanessa

She was loving and kind,
She was always hanging in my mind,
But now she's hard to find . . .

Sleek black hair,
Sitting in her special chair,
But what has happened, we can't repair . . .

She loved to go out for tea,
Much to her glee.
For now she is free . . .

She was our special friend,
But it's not the end,
Forever our love to send . . .

We will always be there by her side
And we have cried,
So now she can glide . . .

But to us she's gold,
Her memories we will hold,
But for now they are cold . . .

Elizabeth Savage (11)
Hornsea Community Primary School, Hornsea

Open Night

The doors open their welcoming arms,
Everyone stares!
Think of a thousand eyes in the night!
My heart beats fast,
The sun fades
And the teacher calls my name.
The time has come,
It is open night.

Ellie Baines (10)
Hornsea Community Primary School, Hornsea

What Would It Be Like To Fly?

What would it be like to fly?
Drifting away, up so high.
Swooping through clouds sprawled out of shapes,
Over the world, mist is draped.
Diving down through atmosphere,
Free as a bird, alone up here.

Elegant as a swan I gracefully glide,
In brilliance and radiance across the deep blue sky.
Below me, the Earth, away it slides,
Peaceful and passive around the sun it flies.

Sweet music, drifts past my ears
And lavender by my nose.
All the planets grin and sneer
As I flutter by, eyes tightly closed.

Cool wind combing my hair,
Floating around in the calm, crisp air.
Arms spread out, feet together.
It's great flying in breezy weather.

Jaya Grady (11)
Hornsea Community Primary School, Hornsea

A Wet Day At The Seaside

Damp sun swims west across the sky,
Whilst the charcoal sea smothers the soft sand.
Clouds as black as bin liners,
Boulders big as buses block the paths.
The groynes, like daggers, stab the horizon -
Slippery with weeds,
Sharp with limpets.
Wet with sea and rain.
We go home.

Harry Garland (10)
Hornsea Community Primary School, Hornsea

My Life As A . . .

Crossbar hanger,
Player watcher,
Huge kicker,
Glove wearer,
Shot saver,
Football puncher,
Post grabber,
Goal stander,
Ball stopper,
Striker frightener,
Penalty diver,
Grass wreaker,
Team relier,
Defender caller,
Free-kick jumper,
Boot tapper,
Corner catcher,
Crowd wilder,
Goal keeper!

Charlie Duckworth (11)
Hornsea Community Primary School, Hornsea

I Think She Saw

The clouds became menacing faces.
The sun drifted away,
Dragging all happiness along with it.
The trees became black claws,
Sleeping houses opened their eyes,
They tiptoed silently,
Along wet, damp alleyways.
She stumbled
And saw . . .

Lucy Turner (10)
Hornsea Community Primary School, Hornsea

Dragon

Strategic fighter
Fire breather
Clean flyer
Dirty wrestler
Spike stabber
Strong swiper
Tail swayer
Massive structure
Heavy glider
Large pounder
Mythical creature
Smooth sailor
Strong swimmer
Tail swiper
Inferno maker
Fire consumer
Consistent stomper
Fat creature
Horny header.

Reece Metcalfe (11)
Hornsea Community Primary School, Hornsea

Sea

Hot sun,
Reflecting on the sea,
Blinds me!
Rock pools,
Brown as toast.
Sand,
Rough as cracked paint,
Its leaping fire blinds me.

Ryan Oxendale (10)
Hornsea Community Primary School, Hornsea

New School
(Inspired by 'Frying Pan In A Moving Van' by Eve Merriam)

I went to a new school this term.
What did you see? Tell, tell, tell.

Well, I saw a rubbish bin with a blue pencil tin.
What else did you see? Tell, tell, tell.

Well, I saw a wobbly chair and a rotten pear
And a rubbish bin and a blue pencil tin.
What else did you see? Tell, tell, tell.

Well, I saw a scruffy boy with his broken toy
And a wobbly chair and a rotten pear
And a rubbish bin and a blue pencil tin.
What else did you see? Tell, tell, tell.

Well, I saw books on the floor and a big black door
And a scruffy boy with his broken toy
And a wobbly chair and a rotten pear
And a rubbish bin and a blue pencil tin.
And that's the last thing I saw at my new school.

Kallum Pinder (11)
Hornsea Community Primary School, Hornsea

Seaside Sun

Dripping watery sun,
Glistening like a torch,
Hangs like fangs in a grey-slate sky.
Water - brown as chocolate,
Foaming - like cappuccino.
Sun creeps into the night.
It is dark.

Megan Smart (10)
Hornsea Community Primary School, Hornsea

The Carnival

It's Carnival weekend.
I can't believe it.
The last time I strolled to the carnival,
It was the best time of my life.

It was just when I stepped forward
And smelt burgers flipping
And potatoes frying.
Heavenly!

I felt fizzy with excitement and hunger.

All that I could see were bright lights everywhere.
Children begging their parents for money.

Hearing the rides playing their cute tunes in the background,
Listening to different bands playing their rocking songs.

So lucky for me, it's that time again.

It's Carnival weekend!
Yippee!

Jessica Henderson (10)
Hornsea Community Primary School, Hornsea

Bees

Bees buzzing like an old fan belt -
Upon a clapped-out motor.
Bees buzzing like tyres on a Lotus.
Stinging!
Busy as a Japanese factory,
Spinning like diablos,
Making honey.

Michael Moffat (10)
Hornsea Community Primary School, Hornsea

Man's Best Friend

Human lover
Cat hater
Bird scarer
Rabbit chaser
Food craver
Bone chewer
Face licker
Tail wagger
Danger warner
Mad barker
Tree climber
Fence jumper
Muck roller
Fur cleaner
Fast runner
Ball catcher
Big cuddler
Loud snorer.

Joseph Bolton (10)
Hornsea Community Primary School, Hornsea

School Day

In the classroom,
The Smartboard wakes -
And blinks into life.
The door shuts like a prison.
Mr Kirke sits . . .
And we are silent,
Looking at a mountain of work,
Cold play - indoors.
Time melts away like a mint.
3.35 - we scuttle home.

Daisy Cox (11)
Hornsea Community Primary School, Hornsea

The Seasons

Spring is the start of life,
And ends the winter gloom.
Days are getting longer,
And flowers start to bloom.

Summer ends the spring,
And welcomes warmth and light.
It makes your smile as golden as the sun,
Summer is such a beautiful sight.

Autumn ends the summer,
When brown, crispy leaves fall.
The nights are getting longer,
As winter is about to call.

Winter ends autumn,
And robins start to sing.
Snow is like a thick, white blanket,
Covering the Earth's skin.

Lily Boocock (11)
Hornsea Community Primary School, Hornsea

Horses

A grey whispering mane.
A colt, smooth as silk.
The grey stallion gallops from the desert horizon,
Past the dancing leaves of the oasis.
The cool breeze splinters the trees!
Across the bronze, sandy plane,
The herd grazes safely.
The night sky hugs the Earth -
Like a blanket.
Clouds pillow the moon.
And they sleep.

Elisha Hodson (10)
Hornsea Community Primary School, Hornsea

Camping

Can't wait, can't wait for the adventure.
Packing the car, shoving everything in,
Tent, sleeping bags, cases, rucksacks,
Cropton Forest, here we come!
Empty the car, pitch the tent.
Hamburgers and mash for tea.
Playing, laughing,
What an adventure!
Shaded by huge enveloping trees,
Watching birds hop on branches,
Listening to squeaks of delight,
This is fantastic!
Every day is so special . . .
Packing the car, shoving everything in,
Tent, sleeping bags, cases, rucksacks.
Can wait, can wait
Don't want the adventure to end.

Louise Johnson (10)
Hornsea Community Primary School, Hornsea

Hornsea Mere

Blue water glistening,
Swans graceful as they open their arms.
Rusty rowing boats,
Floating along the shimmering lake.
Now looks like new glass,
Shimmering wildly.
Now the moon rises boldly
As light turns to dark.
Swans and geese are fast asleep,
Now the moon is covering the lake with a blanket.
The moon turns the lake into a diamond ring at a wedding fayre.

Bethany Hunter (10)
Hornsea Community Primary School, Hornsea

Ocean

The ocean is a blanket,
Deep, dark and cool,
Hiding a thousand mysteries.
Beneath, on the seabed,
Moonlight glistens on the coral . . .
And rainbow-coloured fish -
Dart, dive, disappear.
Huge, thunderous waves crashing loudly
Against the jagged rock,
Whilst the salty foam,
Quietly licks the sand,
Lapping, swirling, swishing.
Gulls search for food,
Far from land,
Hungry mouths to feed in the nest.
And beneath the calm surface of water,
Sit predators, swimming, ready to hunt.

Jack Anthony (11)
Hornsea Community Primary School, Hornsea

Freedom Festival

To the 'Freedom Festival' - I go.
In the crowd - I walk.
To my parents - I return.
In my hand - a poster.
The sun opens its mouth.
The crowd sways and opens its bulging eyes!
On my dad's shoulders - I scream.
As people watch - I stare.
When people move - I stay.
The moon is a trapped lollipop above the clouds.
We go home.

Elsie Stead (10)
Hornsea Community Primary School, Hornsea

Tiny Sneaker

Family lover,
Milk drinker,
Eye blinker,
Noise maker,
Basket sleeper,
Lap sitter,
Toy player,
Ball hitter,
Kitten cuddler,
Wet kisser,
Crazy laugher,
Word speaker,
Nappy filler,
Dolly dreamer,
Pram pusher,
Dummy sucker,
Tiny sneaker!

Angel Farmer (1)
Hornsea Community Primary School, Hornsea

Horse Lover

Fun giver,
Saddle sitter,
Horse rider,
Show jumper,
Dressage hater,
Head kisser,
Mane comber,
Bridal cleaner,
Straw bedder,
Horse lover.

Jade Grantham (11)
Hornsea Community Primary School, Hornsea

Circus

Roll up, roll up, the circus is here.
The children all give a spectacular cheer.
Tickets on sale for a pound and a penny.
'Do you, yes you, want to buy any?'
The 'Big Top' rises up to the sky.
The ringmaster lets out an extremely loud cry.
'Roll up, roll up,' the circus is about to start.
In come the dancing horses and the funny clowns in their old carts.
See the large grey elephant trumpet a sound.
The clowns start to dance around and around.
The acrobat swings from the high rope.
Let's hope he catches the other bloke.
Watch the juggler throw his balls up in the air.
The juggler shouts to the children, 'Join in if you dare!'

'Roll up, roll up,' the circus is coming to an end,
It's time to go home, me and my friends.

Caitlin Musgrave (10)
Hornsea Community Primary School, Hornsea

Legoland

The first ride,
Dragon!
A supersonic spark maker,
Thunders up an endless hill.
The dizzy highs matched only by the deathly plummet.
The fear-induced adrenaline
And *devastating* speed.

Brandon Seaman (11)
Hornsea Community Primary School, Hornsea

Howling Winds

H owling winds deafen children,
U nstoppable rain pierces town,
R unning infants terrified as raging winds rip houses' roofs off,
R uthless stones become airborne,
I ntense rain slowly softens,
C alm winds relieve pedestrians,
A ngry people look at devastation,
N obody has any thoughts of survival,
E verybody is hopeless as help slowly comes.

T ense winds horrify people of all ages,
O nly luck will help them,
R ain batters down as wind sweeps leaves,
N othing gets in the way,
A ll people are shattered,
D oes anybody's house still exist?
O nly they know.

Ryan Postill (10)
Hornsea Community Primary School, Hornsea

The Moon

The moon is a white diamond.
When night falls, it opens its eye,
Comes alive,
Humming,
Glittering,
Glowing,
He smiles at us.

Connor Foster (10)
Hornsea Community Primary School, Hornsea

Loud Barker

Loud barker
Tail wagger
Ball catcher
Bone chewer
Cat hater
Daytime snoozer
Human lover
Sun worshipper
Biscuit eater
Lead follower
Night watcher
Bird chaser
Money chewer
Ear licker
Mouse catcher
Man's best friend.

Kirsten Hobson (10)
Hornsea Community Primary School, Hornsea

Feline Friends

Face licker,
People lover,
Joy giver,
Tummy rubber,
Walk lover,
Mouse chaser,
Snow liker,
Tail sniffer,
Food lover,
Meat eater,
Milk drinker,
Heart warmer.

Bryony Sanson (11)
Hornsea Community Primary School, Hornsea

Lost In The Woods

Was he alone?
It was dark, so dark,
Darker than the grave.
Twigs snapping, owls hooting, wolves howling!
Wild wind blowing trees, swaying them, side to side.
The trees reached out to grab him,
He was trapped,
There was no escape.
Something tapped the stranger.
Who was it? What was it? Where was it?

It was running, running fast,
Bushes stopping it, branches pulling it back.
He was sinking deeper and deeper into squishing mud.
The mud opened its mouth and sucked him in.

He was alone . . .

Josh Myers (11)
Hornsea Community Primary School, Hornsea

A New School

(Inspired by 'Frying Pan In A Moving Van' by Eve Merriam)

I went to a new school this term.
What did you see?
Tell, tell, tell.
I saw a big fat cat and a cricket bat
And a girl having a chocolate bar
And a teacher in a car
And a baseball and I heard a bird's call
And a wooden chair and a big green pear
And a red bin and a black tin.

And that is all I saw at school this term.

Olivia Mortimer (11)
Hornsea Community Primary School, Hornsea

Back To School

(Inspired by 'Frying Pan In A Moving Van' by Eve Merriam)

I went to a new school this term.
What did you see?
Tell, tell, tell.
Well I saw a monkey rubbish bin and a small pencil tin.
What else did you see?
Tell, tell, tell.
Well I saw a piranha fish and a girl called Trish
And a monkey rubbish bin and a small pencil tin.
What else did you see?
Tell, tell, tell.
Well I saw a piranha fish and a girl called Trish
And a monkey rubbish bin and a small pencil tin.

And that's all I saw at my new school.

Kyle Cousins (10)
Hornsea Community Primary School, Hornsea

The Tenth Party

My beautiful birthday banner sways gently in my room,
Balloons wafting in the warm air.
Today is the magnificent day,
My birthday!
Doorbell rings,
Door bursts open,
Guests arrive, laughing and excited.
Ripping my parcels,
Reading my cards,
A wonderful feeling trickles through my body,
Games, dancing, party food,
Guests departing, smiling and tired.
My beautiful birthday banner is still swaying gently in my room.

Chloe Knight (10)
Hornsea Community Primary School, Hornsea

Maisy

My spirited dog's name is Maisy
Although she's often slightly crazy.
She is also *extremely* lazy,
My shaggy dog Maisy.

Dynamic Maisy is mine
For that she is absolutely fine.
Though she doesn't always smell divine
But after a soapy wash she is fine.

Sometimes I call her Maisy-Moo
Particularly when she smells of shampoo!
I wish I had a wonderful life like you,
My gentle, gorgeous Maisy Moo.

Natalie Booth (11)
Hornsea Community Primary School, Hornsea

Anglo-Saxons

Dawn riser
Bee keeper
Muddy worker
Herb gatherer
Cake burner
Story teller
Bread maker
World explorer
Cloth maker
Field plougher
Corn grower
Village guarder
Wood collector
Hunger sufferer.

Chloe May Smith (8)
Hutton Cranswick CP School, Driffield

Disaster!

Cries of joy,
Screams from Hell,
Bravery of firefighters,
Rescue teams
Saving people's lives.

Crashing of buildings,
Falling down to the ground,
Gone in a flash,
No one found.

Annoyed,
Sad,
Worried,
Broken families
Screaming for help!
No one heard.

Thousands of
People hurt . . . like never before,
Hundreds dead
When was this
Wave of madness
Going to end?

Help!
Someone was heard.
Screams of gladness,
Will never end,
One false move,
Someone dead,
One right move,
Someone saved!

Jessica Humble (11)
Hutton Cranswick CP School, Driffield

Disaster!

The sound of screaming and sirens fill the air
The ground shakes as I run down the street
People running, weeping, trying to get to safety
My eyes are full of tears as I slowly fall to the ground
Feeling - nothing at all.

The smell of fear and desperation
The whirlwind right behind me
I fall to the ground and a river of blood
Immediately surrounds me.

Bang!
Help,
Horror,
Volcano,
Run!
The lava chases me endlessly down the village
Running faster and faster
Where's my mum?
Got to find her - *No!*

Quick run . . .
Hide in this building . . .
The ground shakes . . .
The biscuit building collapses on me . . .
A glimpse of light . . .
Then the door opens . . .

Hope?
I see a hand then an arm
Someone is saved
Everybody is happy, like they just won the lottery
One more life saved for good!

Jamie Elliott (10)
Hutton Cranswick CP School, Driffield

Disaster!

Earthquake
Bang!

Cars getting smashed up,
the smell of dust and rubble,
savannahs blaring and screaming,
people running around - as fast as F1 cars,
looking around, houses destroyed,
people lie motionless,
drops of blood fall off my head,
people crying,
shrieks of help,
cries of despair,
happiness - as people come out alive!

Tornado
Whirl!

People, cars and houses getting sucked up,
everything destroyed,
it sweeps round,
spinning round and round,
sucking up things, like a hoover,
no stopping it,
the city - a piece of paper ripped apart,
but after it . . .
in the calm,
people rebuild their lives!

Matthew Watson (10)
Hutton Cranswick CP School, Driffield

Disaster!

Earthquakes
They are devastating
They are upsetting
Silence . . .
Buildings falling down like Lego
Two seconds later . . . rubble and damage
Very noisy
Dust everywhere
People crying - rivers of tears
The sound of sirens . . .
Replaces the silence!

Tornadoes
Extreme winds
Houses falling
Family and relatives dead
People screaming
Children crying
People pulling people out of rubble mountains
Army providing food and shelter
Mums crying seeing their children alive
People injured
Devastation fills the air

Thousands spent on new houses
Years of rebuilding
This is what happens in *natural disasters!*

Lindsay Jordan (10)
Hutton Cranswick CP School, Driffield

Disaster

Silence . . .
Crash
Buildings gone in a flash
Rivers of sadness in the air

Loss is hung in the air
A foggy mist surrounding everyone
Aid and shelter needed more
Damage all around the place
Earthquake traps more and more

Victims stuck under rubble
Cries of help - stuck forever
Broken families everywhere
Running like cheetahs away from the devastation

A sudden shout of hope
Surprised faces all around as
Firemen pull a survivor
Out of the natural disaster
Victims found . . . barely alive

Cries of joy fill the air
A smile - a beam of sunlight in the gloom
Children emerge as orphans
Blankets of arms around survivors
Happiness.

Holly Pickles
Hutton Cranswick CP School, Driffield

Disaster!

Disaster and destruction has hit the Earth
over the life of humans, animals and the faint-hearted.
Earthquakes
Tsunamis
Tornadoes
Volcanic eruptions
Hurricanes
Landslides
And many more.

Earthquakes shake, houses make
Death and destruction.
More are dead.
There are people lying, people crying
And many more will be dying.

An eye-light of sun shines through the gaps in the rubble
A glimpse of hope as someone survives.

Many people still trapped.
Nothing to do but try to *survive!*
Food and water needed
Survivors scavenging for food, in bins and on the streets.
Violence breaks out as people fight for food.
Nowhere to live or sleep.
Disaster!

Oliver Barker
Hutton Cranswick CP School, Driffield

My Dreams

Dreams,
It seems . . .
That they are in your head
And you have them in your bed.

My dream starts in a weird wood
Got to get out of there, I really should
Then there is a rustle in the trees,
'Somebody help me, pretty please!'

Witches and giants came in the night
That was when I had a terrible fright
And there they were . . .
Whispering, 'Get her!'

Then a bright light flashed before their eyes
And they legged it in surprise
Because a fairy appeared out of the blue
And scared the monsters with a single *boo!*

Then the fairy gently said to me,
'It's time to go home now, Mollie.'
She waved her wand and off I flew
And as I went I said, *'Too da loo.'*

Mollie Elliott (8)
Hutton Cranswick CP School, Driffield

Ancient Greek Olympics

Big, heavy, flying plates
Big pointy spears
Muscly men flying all over
In the honour of Zeus
Sweat dripping off foreheads
All competitors were naked.

Bethany Angus
Hutton Cranswick CP School, Driffield

Disaster

People sat at home
Just then . . . disaster strikes
Everyone screams
Sirens screech.

Everything you own
Has gone
Some people are trapped
Unable to move.

Buildings fall
Like dominoes
The smell of devastation
Fills the air.

A week later
People let out cries of joy
As people dearest to them
Get saved.

But the trauma
They've been through
Stays in people's heads
Forever.

Sophie Dennis (11)
Hutton Cranswick CP School, Driffield

Disaster

Crash! Without warning
Big pieces of building fall
From the sky. The taste of
Blood and dust covering your mouth.
It's not a nice feeling to know that
Close relatives and friends are being destroyed
Every second.

People being dug out of the rubble
Bodies lying on the floor
Nobody knows what
To do anymore.

People weeping everywhere
Car sirens fill the air
Screaming people, running round
Ragged, trying to find loved ones.

As firemen fight back fire,
The flame's fingers try to reach out,
Causing more disasters.
Devastation, houses collapse
Like a pack of cards.

Chloe Oxlade
Hutton Cranswick CP School, Driffield

Anglo-Saxons

Viking conqueror
Village attacker
Fierce warrior
Sword fighter
Shield defender
Country settler
House builder.

Sam Peter Dixon
Hutton Cranswick CP School, Driffield

Cyclops

A green beast
A fearsome feast
A one-eyed watcher
He's got ya
Tatty clothes
Don't doze
Lazy lump
Mighty bump
Shin shredder
Tough header
Big horn
Don't mourn
Weapon whacker
He's gonna attack ya
Mean and mighty
Big fighty
Arm breaker
Heels take you

It's Cyclops.

Freya Donohoe
Hutton Cranswick CP School, Driffield

The Minotaur

Big hairy man.
Scary nightmare.
Ancient beast
Scary bear
Hero killer
Half-man
Half-bull
Horror face.

Harry Elstob
Hutton Cranswick CP School, Driffield

Disaster

Crash!
Buildings collapsed
People screaming
Sirens screeching

Bang!
Injured victims
Sadness hung in the air like a shadow
Sirens screeching

Boom!
The roar of engines
Supplies falling like raindrops
People happy
Sirens screeching

Help!
Faint cries from the rubble
Bravery bursting through
Another life saved
Sirens screeching.

Lauryn Drewery (10)
Hutton Cranswick CP School, Driffield

Anglo-Saxons

Wood collectors
Fire makers
Bee keepers
Field ploughers
Iron forgers
Herb gatherers
Egg gatherers
Hog hunters
Anglo-Saxons.

James Lowe (8)
Hutton Cranswick CP School, Driffield

Anglo-Saxons

Field ploughers
Wood collectors
Vegetable growers
Bread makers
Sword sharpeners
Sword fighters
Bee keepers
Cup makers
Marble players
Key holders
World travellers
Anglo-Saxons.

Olivia Bradshaw (7)
Hutton Cranswick CP School, Driffield

Destruction

Disaster, everywhere is sadness
Buildings collapsing on people,
people dying.
Walls collapsing like a pack of cards
that have just been knocked over.
Boom!
Buildings fall to the ground
like smashed plates.
People fall like dominoes.
Pieces of building fall like oversized
toenails.
Disaster!

Connor Hoskins (11)
Hutton Cranswick CP School, Driffield

Disaster

People hurt
People dying
People saved
People sighing
Everyone trying to get to safety
Mothers and fathers worrying
Children orphaned
Scared to death
What's going to happen?
Hearing screams
Cries of panic all around
Scared of what lies ahead.

Lauren Donkin
Hutton Cranswick CP School, Driffield

Minotaur

Strength crusher
Bone brusher
Flesh gulper
Feast finder
Marrow muncher
Blood bowser
Maze home
Giant bull
Human treat
Horn ripper
Ginormous Greek
The Minotaur.

Matteo Penny (10)
Hutton Cranswick CP School, Driffield

Anglo-Saxons

Muddy workers
Boat makers
House builders
Cloth makers
Field ploughers
Corn growers
Village guarders
Wood collectors
Bread makers
Bell ringers
Wax writers
Anglo-Saxons.

Bethany Hoskins (8)
Hutton Cranswick CP School, Driffield

Anglo-Saxons

Dawn riser
Pot maker
Cloth weaver
Fire builder
Cake burner
Stew stirrer
Quern turner
Bread maker
Key holder
Child raiser
Anglo-Saxon woman.

Lucy Richardson (8)
Hutton Cranswick CP School, Driffield

Cyclops

Skull basher
One-eyed starer
Sheep barer
Skull basher
Life smasher
Sheep muncher
Bone cruncher
Two-toed beast
Ten-man feast
Green-skinned monster
He will give you a long stare.

James Beresford (9)
Hutton Cranswick CP School, Driffield

Minotaur

Wall crasher,
Car masher,
Ant stomper,
Meat eater,
Bone smasher,
Blood slurper,
Puppy crusher,
Horns as hair,
No one can stand him,
Because he is a beast,
And he is the Minotaur.

Jordan Macpherson
Hutton Cranswick CP School, Driffield

Cyclops

A sheep stroker
A night stalker
A one-eyed monster

A skull collector
The thing is called Hector
Likes a drink called nectar

Get the muscly factor all right
Don't come across him at night
Likes to fight
It's the Cyclops.

Emma Jane Cuthbert (10)
Hutton Cranswick CP School, Driffield

Cyclops

One-eyed
Club basher
Teeth gnasher
Sheep watcher
Life snatcher
Two-toed
Never foed
Bone musher
Toe crusher
It's a Cyclops.

Noah Hughes-Smith (10)
Hutton Cranswick CP School, Driffield

Olympic Games

Different kinds of events
Great big tents
Flying spears in the air
Watch out for metal plates
Once in four years
Make sure there are no tears
No greedy pigs
It needs to go round
But watch and stare
I am magnificent.

Katie Simpson
Hutton Cranswick CP School, Driffield

Medusa

Reptiles as hair,
No one can bear
The sight of her,
She turns people to stone,
Then they have no bone,
Eyes as hard as gold,
That no one can hold,
Because they are so bold,
Don't go near,
The magnificent man-murderer *Medusa!*

Georgina Griffin
Hutton Cranswick CP School, Driffield

Anglo-Saxon

Dawn riser
Hard worker
Pot maker
Food grower
Animal keeper
Village defender
Hog hunter
Iron forger
Monastery attacker
Dusk retirer.

Aidan Prince (7)
Hutton Cranswick CP School, Driffield

Medusa

A hero's worst nightmare.
An evil stare.
A part of the evil trio.
A fright maker.
A death creator.
A snaky fright.
A horrible sight.
A head full of snakes.
A statue it makes.
A myth to fear.

Eleanor Lowe (10)
Hutton Cranswick CP School, Driffield

Medusa

A snake barer
A scary starer
A creator of nightmares
Say your prayers
Stone carpenter
Are you scared of her?
Two sisters
They look like blisters
She can see yuh
It's Medusa.

Catherine Yates
Hutton Cranswick CP School, Driffield

Anglo-Saxons

Dawn riser
Key holder
Bee keeper
Hay maker
Winter hater
Child raiser
House cleaner
Bread maker
Vegetable grower
An Anglo-Saxon woman.

Melissa Chloe Collins (8)
Hutton Cranswick CP School, Driffield

Anglo-Saxon Men

Viking killer
Sword user
Shield protector
Village guarder
Spear thrower
Vegetable eater
Herb finder
Chicken eater
Norman hater
Anglo-Saxon men.

Joshua Harrison (7)
Hutton Cranswick CP School, Driffield

Anglo-Saxons

Fire makers
Bread bakers
Stew stirrers
Vegetable eaters
Child raisers
Candle makers
Cloth weavers
Key holders
Medicine makers
Winter haters.

Ella Griffiths (8)
Hutton Cranswick CP School, Driffield

Anglo-Saxons

Village guarders
Bell ringers
Floor cleaners
Bee keepers
Boat rowers
Pot makers
Candle makers
Dinner makers
Fire makers
Blanket makers.

Aaron Stephenson (7)
Hutton Cranswick CP School, Driffield

Anglo-Saxons

Early rising
God worshipping
Daily praying
God believing
Bible writing
Manuscript illuminating
Truth telling
Tales sharing
Monastery dwelling
Anglo-Saxon monk.

Abbrielle Steele (8)
Hutton Cranswick CP School, Driffield

Disaster

Lives saved, houses destroyed
People crying rivers of tears
People dying
Lots of noise
Lots of smells

Buildings collapsing like trees felled by the wind
People caught like trapped mice
Waiting for rescuers to free them
Lives saved!

Joshua Yoell
Hutton Cranswick CP School, Driffield

Anglo-Saxons

Bread makers,
Chicken feeders,
Egg gatherers,
Fruit growers,
Bee keepers,
Vegetable eaters,
Animal keepers,
Herb gatherers,
Medicine makers.

Patrick Donohoe (7)
Hutton Cranswick CP School, Driffield

Anglo-Saxons

House builder
Field plougher
Village defender
Sword striker
Bee keeper
Beer drinker
Hunger sufferer
Norman detester
Anglo-Saxon man.

George MacPherson (8)
Hutton Cranswick CP School, Driffield

Anglo-Saxons

Hard working
Wood cutting
Animal hunting
House building
Roof thatching
Mead drinking
Story telling
Anglo-Saxon man.

Tom Matthews (7)
Hutton Cranswick CP School, Driffield

Anglo-Saxons

Story teller
Key holder
Child raiser
Child mourner
Wool gatherer
Spindle twister
Cloth dyer
God worshipper.

Lauren Alice Wilmot (7)
Hutton Cranswick CP School, Driffield

Anglo-Saxons

Sword fighter
World explorer
Village defender
Shield protector
Monastery raider
Country invader
Hunger sufferer.

Rory Garbutt (7)
Hutton Cranswick CP School, Driffield

Anglo-Saxons

Boat makers
Sea sailors
World explorers
Jewel traders
Battle winners
Monastery raiders
Country settlers.

Anna O'Malley (8)
Hutton Cranswick CP School, Driffield

Forgotten

Quiet, unheard whimpers
escape from the dog's mouth.
Frightened on the noisy road
the dog lies there forgotten.

Desperate cries follow
the small trembling cat.
Longing for a loving home,
the cat lies there forgotten.

Aching limbs prevent
the horse from working.
No use to the farmer now,
the horse lies there forgotten.

Abandoned animals sobbing,
homeless, afraid, unloved.
Not being able to fend for themselves,
they all lie there forgotten.

I clench my fists,
my stomach sickening.
Thinking about it day and night,
wishing for it to stop.

Rebecca Sheehan (10)
Ingham Primary School, Lincoln

Winter · Haiku

Friends come round and play
Some hot chocolate, hooray!
Snowball fights galore!

Callum O'Grady (10)
Ingham Primary School, Lincoln

At The Theme Park!

'Hey look at the ride
it's called the 'Shocky Shock'.'

'But I need a rest,
let's sit on that big rock.'

'I am so hungry,
yum, a candyfloss stall.'

'Oh do be careful,
watch out please, do not fall.'

'Hop on this cool ride,
please will you get strapped in.'

'*Ooh,* I'm feeling sick,
can someone see the bin?'

'*Ahh,* please keep me safe,
are you okay yourself?'

'Are you really sure
that this is good for health?'

Ruby Eady (9)
Ingham Primary School, Lincoln

Brushes Of The World

Toothbrush, toothbrush goes in your gob,
Toilet brush, toilet brush goes down the bog.
Paintbrush, paintbrush paint me a picture,
Mop brush, mop brush, mop up the water.
Sweeping brush, sweeping brush with a dustpan,
In a rush with a brush you funny little man.
Hairbrush, hairbrush, don't use it if you're bald,
It is very, very funny, the names a brush can be called.

To be honest, I'd rather use a Hoover!

Joel Ellin (11)
Ingham Primary School, Lincoln

Beautiful Seasons

As spring comes, the plants grow,
The flowers shoot up, row by row,
The green grass, the glistening dew,
The leaves on trees and bushes, everything new.

As summer comes, the sun shines,
The blossoms blow, the colours divine,
Then the leaves will start to fall,
And then, quite slowly, the winds will call.

As autumn comes, the brown and yellow leaves
Flutter down from orange and red trees,
At dusk, beautiful birdies fly
In the dark purple and twilight sky.

As winter comes, the snow will make you shiver,
The temperature freezes up the rivers,
But watch out! Your behaviour must be exquisite,
Because who knows? Maybe Santa might visit!

Matthew Wood (10)
Ingham Primary School, Lincoln

Unfair!

Petrified, he always sobs.
Trying to be brave, he is saving his solitary tear.
It is not funny,
He does not get paid any money!

It's a heartbreaking life,
Chucking seeds for miles on a farm,
He gets really tired.

As the young child walks home,
To see his parents lying on the wooden floor,
He is forced the next morning to go and work again.

Beth Slater (11)
Ingham Primary School, Lincoln

Death Awaits

Ammo scattered around the dusty battlefield,
loud guns shooting and death awaits.
Crawling to cover!
Thinking of a plan to win.

Death awaits!

Families lost, dust blowing across the ground,
crawling with the dust in your face.

Death awaits.

Ammo, bullets and guns.
In the distance seeing black-suited Taliban
walking like they're in a scrum.
British Vs Taliban.

Who will win the war?

Death awaits.

Archie Moyses (10)
Ingham Primary School, Lincoln

Hell And Heaven

Ammo scattered in an old ruined house,
left to rust like a piece of metal.
Taliban soldiers scatter in the dust
like a ghost in snow as an Apache arrives.
Corpses lie on the dusty path to *victory,* no limbs to spare.
Civilians fleeing to an unknown destination.

American reinforcements arrive to back us up, the English.
Taliban dropping like flies.
Soon they're seen as extinct.

Jordan Thorne (11)
Ingham Primary School, Lincoln

The Whale Of The Sea

She spreads herself below the land,
never plain, never bland.
The creatures of the sea swim deep,
some awake and some asleep.
But what is this disgusting muck,
that the walkers of the land just chuck?
Into our depths it stays just there,
how can we tell them - it's not fair?
Their petrifying behaviour makes its mark,
on the hunters that down there lark.
The mean, cruel stink that never goes,
why can't it just leave us alone?
What would you do,
if it was around you?
Would you be like us and cry,
and just sit there waiting for you to die?

Hannah Patrick (11)
Ingham Primary School, Lincoln

What Is The World Without Animals?

What is a tiger without a forest?
What is a gorilla without a tree?
What is a bee without a comb?
What is a panda without bamboo?
What is a polar bear without ice?
What is an elephant without water?
What is a cheetah without its skin?
What is the world without animals?

Hedley Butlin (10)
Ingham Primary School, Lincoln

Orphans

Orphans on the streets feeling invisible,
Wrapped in cold rags.
Probably broken-hearted,
Hoping they are going to be rescued,
A solitary tear runs down their faces.
Nobody cares about them, walking by.
Sun starts to fade away,
Soon it is silent until the next day,
When the same lonely routine starts again.

Crouching in the doorway, staring at children
Spoilt with sweets and ice creams, passing by,
Feeling ashamed and a bit jealous.
Orphans have to find leftover food around the streets or beg . . .
Weaker and weaker!

Grace Hammond (9)
Ingham Primary School, Lincoln

Animal Cruelty

A miserable, upset lion turns and twists in agony.
Millions of glaring faces pressing against the glass,
The lion roars and more noise arouses,
Tired, he slides down and a gunshot is heard.

More and more animals are shoved into the lion's cage,
More and more animals die and are forgotten,
Only lucky ones survive,
And they only have a slim chance.

Thousands more faces press against the glass,
Watching animals suffocate and die.
The confused lion curls up in complete misery,
Waiting to hear his last sound.

Maddie Crossan (9)
Ingham Primary School, Lincoln

The School Trip!

'Hurry up, get on the bus,
Jessica, you should not fuss,
Dave, don't open up your pop,
Libby, don't tell the bus driver to stop!'

'Mrs Clark, I feel really sick,'
'Mrs Edwards, will I see a chick?'
'Jamie, where's your bag?
Ann, sit up straight, don't sag!'

'Mrs Spencer, are we nearly there yet?'
'Bethany don't worry, we're not going to get wet.'
'I love singing, *la, la, la.*'
'Mrs Blackbourne, are we still quite far?'

Isabella Hebborn (10)
Ingham Primary School, Lincoln

The Greyhound Cries

Being used for being fast, the greyhound cries
Terrified, invisible, lonely, the greyhound cries
In pain, confused, the greyhound cries
Thinking, *how did I get here?*

Longing to go, the greyhound cries
Frightened, the greyhound cries
Abandoned, afraid, alone, the greyhound cries
Thinking, *why am I here?*

Can barely cope, the greyhound cries
Anxious, scared, the greyhound cries
Desperate, distraught, the greyhound cries
Thinking, *who sent me here?*

Lucy Thornton (9)
Ingham Primary School, Lincoln

Autumn

Trees are gently swaying.
Summer is all but done,
The grass is old and fraying,
And autumn has just begun.

The big chestnut trees,
Are all rusty and brown,
And everywhere I look, leaves,
One by one flutter down.

The trees are full of colour,
It is autumn once again,
And leaves of red and gold,
Are lying in the lane.

Laura-Alice Wilkinson (11)
Ingham Primary School, Lincoln

Whales

Confused whales swimming in the sea,
frightened where their best mate has gone.
Feeling sad because they feel trapped
and have no freedom from the unfair enemy.
Killing them for absolutely no reason.

Angry whales watching the decks' every sudden move.
The whales wondering when the humans will strike.

Harry Ayrton (9)
Ingham Primary School, Lincoln

Motorbike

A motorway racer
A wheel screecher
A village scarer
A traffic skipper
A law breaker
A curve skimmer
A two wheeler
A noise maker
A flashy whizzer
A trick maker
A mad speeder
A boy racer.

Emma Bailey (9)
Ingleby Arncliffe CE Primary School, Northallerton

Up In The Clouds

A height lover
A speedy traveller
A cloud gnasher
A high flyer
A loud engine
A tarmac lander
A people carrier
A high roarer
A sky flyer
A mile blaster
A sky dasher
A good looker.

Alice Holmes (8)
Ingleby Arncliffe CE Primary School, Northallerton

Helicopter

A super saver
A silly scooper
A glad glider
A life helper
A zooming whizzer
A whirling breaker
A high breaker
A transport whizzer
A slow roarer
A helicopter.

Sam Willey (8)
Ingleby Arncliffe CE Primary School, Northallerton

Skateboard

Street dancer
Trick master
Trendy wheeler
Style maker
Ramp leaper
Park skater
Deck rider
Bone breaker
Reckless rider
Foot worker.

Niamh Newton (11)
Ingleby Arncliffe CE Primary School, Northallerton

Lamborghini

An Italian dream
A sleek machine
A good looker
A street admirer
A street racer
An eye taker
A tarmac crusher
A speedy dream
A flash taker
A time dasher.

Dilan Nash (11)
Ingleby Arncliffe CE Primary School, Northallerton

Train

Station stopper
People carrier
Steamy engine
Cool traveller
Rail basher
Mile gobbler
Whistle blower
Long liner
Loud hooter
Strong puller.

Issebelle Shipman (7)
Ingleby Arncliffe CE Primary School, Northallerton

F1

A fast racer
A speed breaker
An air slasher
A good looker
A tyre screamer
A circuit racer
A shiny breaker
A cool racer

A brilliant breaker.

Mark Porter (10)
Ingleby Arncliffe CE Primary School, Northallerton

Up, Up In The Clouds

A high flyer
A cloud basher
A sky dasher
A height lover
A fab flight
A luxury looker
An air rusher
A mile blaster
A runway roarer.

Holly Dyke (9)
Ingleby Arncliffe CE Primary School, Northallerton

Cruise Liner

Luxury finder
Sea separator
Easy relaxer
Sick maker
Slow chugger
Stress loser
World traveller
Long sinker
Iceberg avoider.

Murdo MacColl (10)
Ingleby Arncliffe CE Primary School, Northallerton

New York

Robins whistling,
Bluebells twisting,
When I went outside I was listening.

I passed the park,
I found a kart,
On my horse I'm a spark.

Up in the sky,
It was high,
Birds were going by.

I saw a tall tower,
Yes, New York!
I enjoyed my day,

Hooray!

Emily Bond (9)
Leadenham CE Primary School, Leadenham

Haunted House

Inside a spooky, scary, haunted house
I pick up a little mouse
Opening a wooden door
I suddenly hear a creak on the floor
Flashing lights fill my sights
Stars that shine so bright
Who fill this sky at night
Looking round I see no sign
Of the house that was mine
Where is the spooky house
And my friend, the mouse?
Darkness is all around me
And now there's no sound.

Shania Rayner (10)
Leadenham CE Primary School, Leadenham

Freedom

The animus of freedom,
Piercing the blissful air,
The wind, as calm as peace itself,
Blowing, everywhere.
The emerald sea of trees below,
Tasting life at last,
The exhilaration of being up there,
High in the heavens vast.
No more gormless gapers gawping,
At your freedom cruelly spent,
Rid of your mind's constraint,
Fly out, as you were meant.

Ben Mott (10)
Leadenham CE Primary School, Leadenham

The Dog

Mouth licker
Food eater
Fast runner
Bark barker
Slobber mouth
Sharp jaws
Meat eater
Slobber jaws
A dog.

Garrett Etheridge (10)
Leadenham CE Primary School, Leadenham

I Am The Tree

I'm the canopy of the land.
In summer I'm clothed
By a range of fruits
And I wear a suit of leaves.

I'm a natural skyscraper,
Home to many creatures.
Sucking water through my feet,
I'm a million years old.

Each branch is a platform of life.
Bark covers my body.
I'm lord of the land,
I used to cover England.

Now my beauty is caged
In small reserves.
In other places where I was,
Chainsaws tolled my ending.

I dread the day when I'm sent to the *sawmill!*

Joe Thurgood (11)
Lutton St Nicholas Primary School, Spalding

The Sea

I am a calm sea.
When boats flow over me,
I jump up and down.
Seaweed tingles inside me.
Fish swim inside me happily.

Then a boat's upon me.
He throws a can of beer inside me.
I lose my temper.
I call in the storm.
I get angrier and angrier.

I get more dangerous
The second his boats rocks.
Finally he falls overboard.
He calls for help.
No one hears him.
Then he drowns.
I'm a peaceful sea.

Ashley Holtz (9)
Lutton St Nicholas Primary School, Spalding

Horse

Galloping through farms
Cantering through fields
Trotting down lanes
Walking into stables
The horse desperately looks for his owner
Hungry, thirsty and cold he searches
Lonely, weak and sad, he gives up
Nearly home, he sees his owner
Next thing, he's safe and sound.

Eryn Davison (10)
Lutton St Nicholas Primary School, Spalding

Shadow

I am your stalker.
I am the ghostly figure that appears
on your bedroom wall at night.
I am your closest friend,
your biggest enemy.
I am your reflection in a different way.
I am dark, not light.
I am only what you make me,
I am what you are.
But some day I will escape.
I will escape from the control,
from the power.
You will never catch me;
I will always be greater
until the sunlight makes me fade away.
But I will always come back . . .

Abigail Curtis (11)
Lutton St Nicholas Primary School, Spalding

The Tree

My roots stand proud. I stand strong.
I have colourful leaves.
They stand out in autumn at sunset.
I'm gigantic, I feel like nothing can destroy me.
My twigs are my weapons. My leaves are my agents.
My apples are my bombs.
I throw bad apples at all people who come to me.
I love it when it rains.
When it's winter, I'm less powerful.
My leaves are gone, apples, too, leaving me with nothing.
That's when people attack me most,
But in the end I'm the winner.

Jordan Turpin (9)
Lutton St Nicholas Primary School, Spalding

107

The Sea

Come and have a tour around the world with me
And see all the different countries.
Cross my barrier and try and find my secret treasure.
People invading my battlefield.
Listen . . . the dreadful sound of creatures drowning below me.
Surfboards digging into me like serrated knives.

Squashed against my barrier; my waves flood cities and towns.
What was that . . . ?
Someone just threw a can of beer into my tummy!
I got really angry and called in the storm.
Some of the men fell overboard.
The sound of the men drowning filled my ears.
After a split second, they had drowned
And bubbles rose to the surface.

Emma Barber (11)
Lutton St Nicholas Primary School, Spalding

A Polar Bear

I'm a key to the North Pole.
People think I am adorable,
I love eating whales but sometimes people
and other polar bears fight me for them.

People are destroying my habitat,
they are creating global warming.
Me and my polar bear friends are being hunted.
I will get my own back.
If they set a foot on me they will be up against
a set of hidden, furry, serrated claws.

Some people get too close
and I always catch them,
I am too fast for Man.

Charlotte Tappenden (9)
Lutton St Nicholas Primary School, Spalding

Tree

I'm a natural skyscraper, a tall glory.
Lichen-jacketed, green and brown.
I stand tall as the sky, looking down on all.
Green-haired, root-footed.

Birds land on me and peck holes in my trunk.
Each branch is a myriad of life.
They think I'm a wooden wonder.

Now I am that no more.
I was cut down and burned.
I pollute the air I once helped
And am reduced to ashes.

Lewis Taylor (10)
Lutton St Nicholas Primary School, Spalding

The Sea

I have yellow blinding lights shining on me.
I'm wounded by ships.
I'm used as a battleground.
I'm vicious - I kill people every day.
I shove them on the rocks.
I'm as green as grass, full of seaweed.
I am king of the world.
In the past I was blue.
I had multicoloured fish peacefully swimming in my tummy.
I have coral reefs in my heart.
The fish eat the plankton.

Luke Morris (9)
Lutton St Nicholas Primary School, Spalding

The Sea

I am the sea.
I'm the most powerful thing on Earth.
I provide homes for scores of millions of fish and animals.

Those humans are like midgets to me,
But they still poison me with their dirty rubbish.
I'm glad if they die in me; it serves them right.
They don't have a brain to know if you sail on me,
I'll keep your jewels.

Ewan Mears (9)
Lutton St Nicholas Primary School, Spalding

Polar Bear

I am as soft as a teddy bear but very violent and aggressive.
Cute as a baby but I strike, seal's dead!
I have claws as sharp as daggers but I have not got much food.
I disguise myself as snow.
The ice caps are melting.
I'm as cold as ice.
Global warming is my worst enemy.
I roar like a lion!

Andrew Cotton (10)
Lutton St Nicholas Primary School, Spalding

The Shore

Tides soak my golden sand,
Leaving a myriad of irresistible sea
livers and beautiful coloured
patterned shells as my treasure.
Then selfish, troublesome creatures
steal my possessions.
This leaves me with nothing,
until another day of new admirable treasures.

Georgina Larham (10)
Lutton St Nicholas Primary School, Spalding

Cool Cheetah

I saw a cheetah like an athlete
Sprinting across the land,
He started doing a handstand.
He dodged around in a smooth kind of way,
But sometimes he missed his prey.

He bites meat like a sassy shark,
But then he saw a lark.
He is very strong,
But sometimes he does something wrong.

He is as fast as lightning
And so good at fighting.
The cheetah has got lasers in his eyes,
But sometimes he lies.

Sometimes he likes to run
And sometimes he likes to have fun.
Deadly killer of Africa!

Bavneet Kang (9)
Netherleigh & Rossefield School, Bradford

German Shepherd

I saw a glimmering vision,
It took my breath away,
'Twas the silhouette of a Shepherd
More regal than words can say.

The beams of light they danced
On a coat of endless black.
Vision of perfection
Atop an iron back.

He stood as a stature
For all the world to see,
What a vision of perfection
The German Shepherd can be.

The look of a noble prince,
Lord of all he surveys,
Confident in himself,
Fixed in aristocratic gaze.

I shall never forget
The vision I saw that day,
Of the mighty Shepherd
Who took my breath away.

Radhika Pamma (10)
Netherleigh & Rossefield School, Bradford

The King Cobra

S ly and slimy
N ever seen
A ttacks suddenly
K ills like an assassin
E ats as it pleases.

Sahd Mahmood (9)
Netherleigh & Rossefield School, Bradford

The Tiger Poem

Majestic tiger
Strides with pride,
With teeth so long
And eyes so wide.

Triumphant tiger,
Striped orange and black,
With his paw
He'll give you a whack.

Horrific tiger
Eats its prey,
The jungle is his kitchen,
He has a feast every day.

Vulnerable tiger,
Last of its kind,
Poachers are out there
Looking for all they can find.

Moiz Raja (9)
Netherleigh & Rossefield School, Bradford

The Killer Lion

A lion, king of all wildlife,
Teeth like a knife,
Kills like a mad bear,
Kills all meat with no care,
Fast like a cheetah,
He's a lucky lion.

L ion, large and ferocious
I t can make death like Hell
O n the side of his head he has a mane
N ext to the tiger he is fierce.

Hassan Khan (9)
Netherleigh & Rossefield School, Bradford

My Cheetah Poem

Cheetahs are fast
Cheetahs are neat
Cheetahs are active throughout the week.

Cheetahs are smart
Cheetahs are cool
Cheetahs are not easy to fool.

Cheetahs play
Cheetahs run
Cheetahs know how to have fun.

Cheetahs laugh
Cheetahs cry
They run so fast they almost fly.

Cheetahs kill
Cheetahs eat
Cheetahs love to lick their feet.

Amaara Noor-Mundiya (10)
Netherleigh & Rossefield School, Bradford

Persian

P uurrrrfect pedigree pussy!
E legant and enchanting like Snow White
R oyal, radiant and relaxed
S haggy, the cat is like a woolly mat
I ntelligent and independent
A dorable but not always available
N ice and occasionally naughty, but only when chasing
    small and sneaky mice!

Oh, my Persian cat, you are so nice!

Hadiya Ashraf (9)
Netherleigh & Rossefield School, Bradford

Cat Poem

The cat is big and ginger and has lots of fur,
When you stroke it, it loves to purr.

The cat lives in a warm house
Where he's sitting on his cosy couch,
Whilst he's on the lookout for a fat mouse.

When he spots the fat mouse
He slyly leaps like a leopard
And pounces on it with his deadly paws,
And then come forward the claws.

The cat likes to play with a ball of wool,
Especially when his tummy is nice and full.

Finally it's time for his nap,
So purring away,
He goes to his owner's lap.

Aminah Khan (10)
Netherleigh & Rossefield School, Bradford

My Cat

C atches mice with its sharp claws
A nd every time the doorbell rings he races to the door
T ough Tiger wants to go to bed. He always shakes his head.

My cat is called Tough Tiger,
But he acts like a cheetah.
His teeth are sharp as daggers.
Really, he is a food nagger.

Asim Shabir (10)
Netherleigh & Rossefield School, Bradford

My Rabbit

My rabbit, Flopsy, is furry and grey,
He hops and walks around all day.
He's just a rabbit but I don't care,
He's so special, so I won't share.
He stands up tall on his short back legs
And twitches his nose when he sees some pegs.
He wiggles his tiny fluffy tail
And runs as fast as he can to the mail.
He is as silent as a quiet mouse
But jumps around happily around the house.
He listens quietly with his floppy ears
Until he makes sure the area clears,
Then he goes back slowly like a snail,
Sneaking carrots and doesn't fail,
Then goes hopping back into his hutch.

Saeed Azam (10)
Netherleigh & Rossefield School, Bradford

My Animal Poem

In Antarctica,
Where the ice is as white as milk,
The penguin walks with grace,
Up and down, from place to place.

When it comes to catching its prey,
It won't let anything get in its way.
With a coat that's as black as the night,
And wide eyes as bright as the light,
It finds the perfect target to eat
With its fine and sharp beak.

It attacks the fish,
This becomes its favourite dish.

Isbah Munir (9)
Netherleigh & Rossefield School, Bradford

Egypt

Special secret afterlife,
Hot gold sand,
Special gods.
Weird hieroglyphs,
Massive pyramids,
Blue water (River Nile).
Dead, scary and smelly mummy,
Terrifying tombs.
Horrible bread,
Biting spiders,
Special treasure,
Boiling hot sun.

Matthew Seedhouse (8)
Norton Free CE Primary School, Sheffield

The Wonderful Ancient Egypt

Hot, sandy desert,
Deep blue River Nile,
Happy, beautiful afterlife,
Spooky, silent mummy,
Magnificent, colourful sarcophagus,
Soft, squishy sand,
Disgusting, stony bread,
Fantastic, almighty pharaohs,
Scary, freaky tombs,
Difficult, hard hieroglyphs,
Tall, green papyrus,
Dark, dangerous pyramids.

Kaylie Chappell (7)
Norton Free CE Primary School, Sheffield

The Wonders Of Ancient Egypt

Horrid, scary mummies,
Amazing, dark pyramids,
Deep, long River Nile,
Pretty sarcophaguses,
Hot, sunny desert.
Super-nasty pharaohs,
Warm, spooky tombs,
Cold linen bandages,
Great, fantastic hieroglyphs,
Clean, purifying and washing,
High green papyrus.

Eleanor Thompson (7)
Norton Free CE Primary School, Sheffield

Egyptian Objects And Places

Frightening, scary sarcophagus,
Scorching hot desert,
Wet, blue River Nile,
Pretty, colourful pharaoh,
Great, lovely death mask,
Horrible, gory mummy,
Green, useful papyrus,
Wood and string toys,
Weird, special hieroglyphs,
Dark, terrible pyramid,
Flat, dry houses.

William Waterhouse (7)
Norton Free CE Primary School, Sheffield

Precious Things About Pyramids

Spooky, pitch-black,
Scary, sparkly sarcophagus,
Ice-cold, buried food,
Up to Heaven, steep stairway,
Scary old body,
Swaying soft sand,
Spooky old Canopic jars,
Shimmering, shiny silver,
Glimmering, glittery gold,
Dazzling glittery jewels.

Amy Bottomley (8)
Norton Free CE Primary School, Sheffield

The Wonders Of Ancient Egypt

Mummified mummy,
Hot, sandy desert,
Green, hard papyrus,
Scary, dark sarcophagus,
Perfect, fantastic pharaohs,
Running River Nile,
Amazing, interesting hieroglyphs,
Scary, super afterlife,
Cold, scary tombs.

Freddie Elam (7)
Norton Free CE Primary School, Sheffield

The View Of Ancient Egypt

Deep, blue River Nile,
Dark, spooky pyramids,
Bright, colourful pharaohs,
Lonely, terrifying mummies,
Tricky, detailed hieroglyphs,
Surprisingly happy afterlife,
Spiky, green papyrus,
Black, frightening sarcophagus.

Molly Raynor-Garside (8)
Norton Free CE Primary School, Sheffield

The Wonders Of The Great Pyramids

Lonely, dark pyramid,
Cold, shimmering gold,
Dead, scary sarcophagus,
Sad, spooky mummies,
Beautiful, shiny crystals,
Super smooth silver,
Spooky, famous pharaohs,
Frightening, old tombs.

Lydia Mia Pass (8)
Norton Free CE Primary School, Sheffield

Egyptian Tombs

Nice and beautiful paintings,
Lovely and great hieroglyphics,
Dark and spooky tombs.

Big and massive pyramids,
Colourful, metal sarcophagus,
Horrid and stinky mummies.

Fraser Cuthbert (7)
Norton Free CE Primary School, Sheffield

A View Of Ancient Egypt

Hot, sandy desert,
Deep, blue River Nile,
Spooky, dead mummies,
Clean, shiny tombs,
Old, yellow pyramids,
Hard, confusing hieroglyphs,
Gold and silver death masks,
Famous, fabulous pharaohs.

Jak Abbey (7)
Norton Free CE Primary School, Sheffield

Hard Hieroglyphs

Lovely, colourful paints,
Perfect, pretty paintings,
Fantastic girl goddesses,
Glorious, great gods,
Amazing, wonderful writing,
Dark, scary pyramids,
Ancient, brilliant scribes,
Sad slaves.

Kathryn Schoon (7)
Norton Free CE Primary School, Sheffield

The Wonders Of Ancient Egyptians

Lonely, spooky mummies,
Scary, deep pyramids,
Hot, sandy desert,
Dark blue River Nile,
Powerful, super pharaohs,
Ancient, happy afterlife.

Lucy Camm (8)
Norton Free CE Primary School, Sheffield

The Ancient Egyptians

Special goldy sarcophagus,
Stinky, freaky mummies,
Green, triangled paypyrus,
Dark yellow tombs,
Colourful, great hieroglyphs,
Famous, fabulous pharaohs,
Wavy, deep, dark River Nile.

Korben Crosby (7)
Norton Free CE Primary School, Sheffield

Egyptian Sarcophagus

Yucky, dead body,
Shiny gold,
Cold masks,
Tall, sandy pyramids,
Rotten, smelly bodies,
Dark black sarcophaguses.

Francesca Hutchinson (7)
Norton Free CE Primary School, Sheffield

Seasons

S pring buds sprouting, peeking through
E ggs decorated, showing life that's new
A ll the lush green fields bask in the sun
S ummer faces happy, excited, having fun
O pulent colours of autumn in all their splendour
N ight skies alight, Guy Fawkes to remember
S now is falling thick and fast, Christmas is coming
    at long, long, last.

Franki Callard (10)
Pannal Primary School, Harrogate

A Night Walk

Wind whistling
Wolves howling
Owls hooting
Are the sounds I get
From the night walk

Trees towering
Fingers pricking
Clouds dull
Are the sights I get
From the night walk

Fresh grass
Thin air
Burning fire
Are the smells I get
From the night walk

Cold air
Woolly gloves
Rough grass
Are the feelings I get
From the night walk

Damp earth
Purple blackberries
Dry leaves
Are the tastes I get
From the night walk

The night walk began
And now has ended
Everyone goes home and
Treats themselves to
A warm hot chocolate.

Lizzie Turcan (11)
Pannal Primary School, Harrogate

All Aboard

Here I am standing all alone,
Nobody to care, nobody to phone.
While I wait here for a train,
The heavens above me begin to rain.
Still I stand on platform 9 and ¾,
My luggage is heavy, where are the porters?
When suddenly the loudspeakers say,
'People waiting, there is a train coming this way.'

I open my eyes, I open them wide,
As my arms dangle loosely by my side.
I can hardly contain all my gladness,
The announcement has washed away all my sadness.
Now the train is coming to a stop,
My heart is racing, about to pop.
'All aboard,' the driver cries,
The loneliness inside me dies.

The train is long, cosy and red,
It won't be long before I'm asleep in bed.
As I snuggle into my seat,
A woman comes by and offers me something to eat.
I say, 'Yes, Madam, I'll take sushi please.'
She replies, 'Did you know that's Japanese?'
Then she leaves, this is the start of my adventure,
I will open the door and I will venture,
Venture a world that I can explore,
I never again will need or want more.

A man comes past and says, 'Egypt lies ahead,'
Before we stop he makes my bed,
But as I'm not tired, I open my door
And decide to walk out to explore.

First I go to the door on my right
And when I go in, well . . . what a sight.
There is a baby sleeping and a mother sighing,
And no wonder there is a small child crying.

Then the mother notices I'm there,
She gives me a smile as she fingers her hair.
Then I wave and shoot out of the door,
I haven't met everyone, there must be more.
I travel along the winding corridor,
As I see an interesting door.
If I open it, what will I find?
The people inside, will they be kind?

The door, I notice, is monstrous and gold
With a sign on it that is big and bold.
On it says *'Royalty inside'*,
It looks like I'm in for an interesting ride.
As I hold my breath, walk forward and enter,
The room is vast as a city centre.
To my surprise, by the light of the moon,
Who's that sipping tea, is it Tutankhamun?

I quickly step back and make my retreat,
I run fast as I can back to my seat.
I am now on an adventure so great,
What possibilities do await?
I feel safe on the Poetry Express,
And no longer feel I need to impress.
Now everyone can clearly see
I'm now as happy as can be.

Ashleigh Henry (11)
Pannal Primary School, Harrogate

Bermuda Triangle

Dear Diary,
I'm all alone on the wide, wide sea,
Except the captain and me.
I'm looking out of the porthole window,
Watching the water swirling below.

All at once the murky blue water clears,
'Land ahoy!' is the message I hear,
And it is true what the captain screeches,
For all of a sudden I saw those beaches.

The great big palm trees standing in the sand
Had huge round coconuts and
The little children playing in the grasses,
A cheek monkey steals a small girl's glasses.

Watching the water lapping against the boat
Makes me shudder and reach for my coat.
I knew that this boat was broken and wrong,
It's amazing that it's still taking us along!

But as the boat sails nearer and nearer,
It seemed to me that it got clearer and clearer
That our tiny boat couldn't get that far,
That island was too far away, too far.

Captain tossed a rope that caught on the ground,
But those strong currents swooshed all around.
The rope slackened in his great hands,
We were tugged away from those golden lands.

The waters were dark and scarily frightening,
There was a thunder clap and bright lightning!
We were getting sucked into a whirlpool.
I screeched and screamed at the sea so cruel!

The wind howled loud in my ears,
My face was stiff with seawater and tears.
The little boat fell apart, as it would,
I hauled myself onto a plank of wood.

Salty brine clogging up my throat,
As I clung on tight to the remains of the boat.
I screamed and I shouted, tearful and feared,
But that was all before I disappeared.

The Bermuda Triangle sucked me in
And now I'm here, that's where I've been.
I lie here at the bottom of the seabed,
I lie here waiting, waiting, but dead.

I'm all alone in the wide, wide sea,
Except a very dead captain and me.
I'm looking out of the porthole window
Watching the water above, not below.

Alice Lavender (11)
Pannal Primary School, Harrogate

Limericks

We have a pet cat called Holly,
Who's nothing like my bro', Olly,
He goes to school,
She sleeps as a rule,
As well as being scared of a brolly.

There once was a boy called Bisty,
His football was said to be nifty,
He played at right back
And sometimes in attack,
And continued till he was fifty.

Ruby is our pet snake,
Her skin is definitely not fake,
We feed her on mice.
To her they taste nice,
How disgusting, for goodness' sake!

Christian King (11)
Pannal Primary School, Harrogate

Beast

The sheds stir and writhe
As whispers rasp around.
The deathly darkness consumes the dozing trains,
The dancing shadows wail like howling wolves . . .

It tears down the grimy track
Spraying up clouds of twirling dust.
Its wheezing fumes are rattling the heather,
Making its scraggly subjects bow.

Swirling sky
Where spirits fly;
Bold stone,
Grey as bone;
Lightning flashes,
Bracken thrashes,
Heather prances, waltzes, dances.

A blustery gale creeps over hills,
Clearly seizing my mirth.
Demonic eyes pierce the dark,
Glaring eerily at me.

Crickets cry,
Trees jive;
Leaves stunt
To the wind's grunts;
Birch leaves skip,
Rowans whip;
Stars wink
As the moon blinks.

Surging through forests, crashing through towns,
The beast is coming, the beast is here.
Can't you see it? It's crystal clear!
It's thundering, blundering, smashing and crashing,
The train beast is here!

Jacques Haddleton (11)
Pannal Primary School, Harrogate

Travel To Camp

My heart is pumping like I'm being chased by hunters.
I get on the train and put my camping gear on the rack.
I sit down by myself, waiting for friends.
The train moves and I'm nervous, however very excited,
And no need to worry as my friends are beside me.
On the way, all I can hear is 'clickety-clank' in my ears
And I am wondering when we will get to camp.
Finally we get off and it's going to be a great weekend.

Philip Mitchell (11)
Pannal Primary School, Harrogate

A Night To Remember

First I went to Pizza Express
My friend, Bronwen, wore a bright blue dress

As the rain outside poured down
I felt that I might make a frown

But I am truly thrilled about tonight
Expecting massive displays of light

Walking along the muddy grass
Looking at the people amass

Finally we arrived at the bonfire display
The location was The Stray

My hands now utterly frozen
Why didn't I wear the gloves my mum had chosen?

The fireworks made a loud sound
I'm glad that my family was around

Blue, gold, red and green
What striking colours I have seen

The bonfire flames went up high
It nearly made little Wilf cry

The ash flying at the crowd
They yell and shout, it's really loud

Smoky embers and gunpowder smells in the sky
Reminding me of past years gone by

Bonfire Night must come to an end
I'm really sad to say bye to my friend

But there's always next year's display
To look forward to after summer's long holiday.

Mabel Calvert (10)
Pannal Primary School, Harrogate

All Aboard The Poetry Express

A nother day on the Poetry Express
L oving the job
L oving each moment

A lways ready for what is coming
B ig obliterating monsters destroying the track
O r fairies and goblins aligning the path
A ll the way to the city it is placed
R ight in the middle of the world of Tavied
D idn't you know? Well I'll show you!

T iming is perfect, we set off on time
H ow do we get there?
E ventually we knew!

P eople singing sets off the tracks
O nly that can take it away
E ven if quiet, anything will do, just keep it ongoing to
   keep monsters at bay
T oobles that bite and Rilbs that sting
R ibes that screech and Xrras that growl
Y undles that pounce and Grillions that prowl

E ven you will get used to it, soon you will know all
X mingles sing and Fingles dance, oh, we've arrived
P eculiar creatures crawl from the rocks
R eligious creatures applaud from the box
E nding the day with a job well done
S oon you forget about the Poetry Express
S uch a wonderful thing to be turned into a mess.

Benjamin Sumner (11)
Pannal Primary School, Harrogate

131

The Mermaid Of Death

Jack the Ripper, 1888,
Was the worst killer - that's no debate!
But all the deaths in that time
Were not his, they were mine.

Will placed a bet of which he was sure
That nobody dies in Lake Winimoore,
But if only he could truly see
What lies in his destiny.

He rowed out into the night,
With the stars shining bright.
The lake made not a sound
As the mermaid swam around.

My scaly hand grabbed the boat,
Leaving poor Will drifting afloat.
I dived into the murky water,
Making Will's life shorter and shorter.

For I am the Mermaid of Winimoore,
Seeking death on the shore,
But all along, can't you see?
All Jack's deaths belonged to me!

Beth Rennie (10)
Pannal Primary School, Harrogate

The Terror-Filled Train Ride

Waiting.
Excitement and terror
Mixed together.
The train arrives,
We squeeze inside.
With a lurch, we're off.

Pitch-black like a tunnel,
Slowly getting faster.
People scream as we whizz round corners.
Brilliant lights show terrifying images,
Graveyard bones?
Pumpkin patch Halloween?
Bats, vampires!
A howl far off, a scream nearby,
More screams, more corners.
All at once, bright sunshine.
Slowing down,
Calming down,
Relief.

'Could we go on the bumper cars next?'

Grace Burns (10)
Pannal Primary School, Harrogate

The Poetry Express

You have to be quiet
And stand right here,
To hear the train coming,
It's coming so near.
Building up steam
And building up power,
It can be seen through the greatest snow shower.
Roaring like a lion,
Racing like a horse,
The great train is coming,
It's coming so close.
Spurting out rhymes
And spilling out verses,
Poems for all,
Even doctors and nurses!
The train rumbles on,
The words keep on churning,
Children of all ages
Are laughing and learning.
And as the train chugs away,
The children are left with plenty to say!

Hannah Mason (11)
Pannal Primary School, Harrogate

Archery

A rrows racing, cutting, chasing
R ows and rows of archers bracing
C ircles on the target calling
H igh in the sky the arrows falling
E agle-eyed they aim for gold
R apid fire like knights of old
'Y es,' he shouts, 'a bullseye.'

Jonah Potter (11)
Pannal Primary School, Harrogate

The Doom Train

The doom train is coming,
It's coming for you,
It's come out of nowhere,
It's come out of the blue!

Bashing, smashing, crashing its way,
The doom train is coming, and you are its prey!

Vampires, mummies, werewolves and more,
Oh no, they've seen you, quick, slam the door!
You've just about made it, but they know where you are,
And if you try to escape, you'll never get far.

The doom train is coming, it's now very near,
Your heart's pumping hard, it's all you can hear!

The engine is dying, morning is here,
The monsters are fading, so is your fear.
You open the door, take a breath of fresh air,
And forget all about that dreadful nightmare.

Jack London (11)
Pannal Primary School, Harrogate

The Winter

T he sound of the crunch under my feet as I walk on the frost
H ear the red-breasted robin singing across the lands
E bony coal eyes sat upon the icy snow of my snowman

W histling wind in my ears, they're almost dropping off
I mmensely icy wind, gnawing at my face
N umerous icicles hanging off my windowpane
T ightly my scarf is wrapped round my neck
E legantly I step out and breathe in the cold air around me
R esting by the coal fire, all warm and comfy, a great day in
the winter.

Rosie Pawson (10)
Pannal Primary School, Harrogate

The Poetry Express

The whistle blows
The engine chugs
To another faraway land

Puffs of smoke come out the fire
All the children have fun
For the train that they desire

The ticket man comes round and round
No one being caught or found

Mums and dads have their coffee
Children stuffing their faces with toffee

Eventually they come to a stop
All the children ready to hop
Off the Poetry Express.

Philip Milsom (10)
Pannal Primary School, Harrogate

A Mighty Ride!

P ast the rivers and through the lakes
O ver mountains and under hills
E njoy dinosaurs back in time
T iny ants but ticklish claws
R oaring lions with gigantic manes
Y awning monkeys with aching limbs

E ntire nations of panthers and snakes
X tra music with xtra drums
P raising priests of Aztec gods
R elaxed children are very tired
E xcited till now, yet ready for
S leep
S leep.

Robert Woods (11)
Pannal Primary School, Harrogate

Runaway Train

The runaway train is rising again,
The runaway train is going faster,
And faster, faster, faster, faster, faster,
Stop!

The wheels screeching on the dusty line,
The sparks flying as fast as time,
The wind is whistling on the dusty black,
I think it's time they turned back.

The runaway train has risen again,
He ran away after that,
And speaking of which, he never came back,
But if he does try to get us again,
Hopefully it won't be the same.

Lucy Fairhurst (10)
Pannal Primary School, Harrogate

Choo, Choo, The Train Is Coming

Chug, chug, the sound of the train
Is like a song on repeat.
Hoot, hoot, goes the whistle,
The next station comes in view.
Passengers stand up, the train stops,
Swoosh, a gust of air blows in,
The doors open.
Some people step off as others climb up.
'Fares please,' shouts the conductor,
Clicking his ticket box as he sells.
Toot, toot, rattle, rattle,
Off we go again,
The journey never ends.

Ben Smith (11)
Pannal Primary School, Harrogate

A Raging Abscess

It's a thumping pain,
Throb, throb and *throb,*
But what could it be?
Thump, thump and *thump.*

I wake up in the night
And wow, I got a fright!
It's hotter than Earth's core itself,
Like a cup of hot soup, sizzling away,
Rage, rage and rage,
A purple pain searing through my head,
But what do I gain?
Nothing but pain.
Thung, thung and *thung.*

Throb, throb and *throb,*
It's almost a tooth.
Bang, bang, bang,
Barging its way,
Tang, tang, tang
Through my gum,
And with that . . .
Man, it was a night
When I got that fright!

Rosie Taylor (10)
Pannal Primary School, Harrogate

The Deadly Dragon

The dragon was green and gold
He was a marvellous sight
His body was strong and bold
And he came out in the middle of night.

Below him in the local town
The people were filled with dread
As the dragon flew over and looked down
He realised that most were dead.

Looking here and over there
Hissing from his forked tongue
He left the town completely empty
Knowing his work there was done.

Jack Ward (10)
Pannal Primary School, Harrogate

Untitled

All aboard the Poetry Express.
I got on the train, I was so impressed.

The steam engine was going
And the atmosphere was flowing.

The people were jolly,
And then came the waitress with the trolley.

The scenery was amazing,
As the sun was glazing.

I set foot off the train
And then it started to rain.

George Gardner (10)
Pannal Primary School, Harrogate

The Castle

Up the hill
The castle looms up above me,
Its stone walls
Pushing me back to the hillside
Where the wolves howl
In their packs.

I walk alone
On the icy, cold path
Freezing my aching feet.

They go
On
And
On;

The door opens
And the warmth of a fire
Drifts towards my
Frozen features and comforts me.

If I come
To your door,

Let me in,
Let me in,
Let me in.

Louise Page (10)
St John's CE Primary School, Brighouse

The Ship

The ship is a broken-hearted boy,
Sad, smashed and scared.
The ship is a lonely lamb.
The ship is a frightened deer.

Faye McCarthy (11)
St Margaret Clitherow's Catholic Primary School, Middlesbrough

The Ship

The ship is a tiny animal, alone
On the swirling, whirling sea.
Destroyed but determined,
It searches for help and protection.
Wailing loudly, it is sadly unheard by anyone
Over the crashing of the waves.
The ship is a helpless creature,
Desperately trying to escape
The sea's tearing claws.

Ciara McGeary (10)
St Margaret Clitherow's Catholic Primary School, Middlesbrough

The Shipwreck

The ship is like a cat
Thrown into a dog's cage,
Destroyed and devastated.
It's like an enemy plane being shot down.
It crashes through the waves,
Trying to resist them.
The ship's a stricken person
Panicking in the perilous waves.

Daniel Barratt (11)
St Margaret Clitherow's Catholic Primary School, Middlesbrough

The Ship

The ship is a helpless, wounded monster,
Dim, dark, dangerous,
Like a destroyed heart.
Suffering ship.
The ship is a dying soul.

Emily Fisher (10)
St Margaret Clitherow's Catholic Primary School, Middlesbrough

The Ship

The ship is an angry monster
Crashing against the cliffs.
The ship is like a cracked-up plate
Smashing and breaking to pieces.
Watching as the people try to escape
And moans for help.
The ship is a lonely monster
With nowhere to go.

Emily Haslam (10)
St Margaret Clitherow's Catholic Primary School, Middlesbrough

The Forfarshire

The ship is an abandoned child,
Helpless and hurt.
It is like a lost animal getting attacked
By a fierce creature.
Dying silently, it cries for help
But is unheard
Above the deadly sound of the sea.
The ship is a warrior who has lost his pride.

Faye Matthews (10)
St Margaret Clitherow's Catholic Primary School, Middlesbrough

The Ship

The ship is a broken soul,
Abandoned, alone.
It is like a twisted mind,
Left with no words to think.
As the dancing waves surround the wreck
The ship is floating like a still body.

Jordan Feher (10)
St Margaret Clitherow's Catholic Primary School, Middlesbrough

The Lighthouse

The lighthouse is a bright light
Glowing in the darkness.
Bold and bright, it shines all night.
It is like a bright beam in
The darkness from above.
The lighthouse is a safe haven,
Clearing the way for the ships at night -
What a light!

Harrison Kent (10)
St Margaret Clitherow's Catholic Primary School, Middlesbrough

The Stricken Ship

The ship is a crying baby whale,
Struggling in the mist for help,
Helpless and hurt.
It is like a human being
Dragged to their death.
Rocking and rolling like an old man
Staring down the street.
The ship is a screeching wolf.

Chloe Gregory (10)
St Margaret Clitherow's Catholic Primary School, Middlesbrough

The Stricken Ship

The ship is a hungry animal,
Starving and solemn.
It is like a lion chasing its prey,
Crying in hunger for a meal.
The ship is an abandoned child
Sobbing for its parents.

Charlie Tilley (11)
St Margaret Clitherow's Catholic Primary School, Middlesbrough

The Ship

The ship is a drowning person.
The boat is a wooden worry.
It crashes like a car crash.
The boat is shaking
Like the water underneath.
The boat is like a cliff
Falling down on someone.

Lydia Hart (9)
St Margaret Clitherow's Catholic Primary School, Middlesbrough

The Stricken Ship

The ship is a person who has lost their love,
Worried and weak,
It's like a broken heart, bleeding and dying,
Reaching out for the love
That will never return.
The ship is a person
Looking for never-ending love!

Grace Wakelin (11)
St Margaret Clitherow's Catholic Primary School, Middlesbrough

The Forfarshire

The ship is an injured fish
Getting attacked by a shark.
Devastated and damaged
It is like a girl stranded
On a desert island.
Drowning in the perilous waves,
The ship is a lonely soul.

Matthew Barry (10)
St Margaret Clitherow's Catholic Primary School, Middlesbrough

The Stricken Ship

The ship is a tennis ball
Being smashed around the court.
Screaming and shouting,
It is like a helpless victim
Being dragged into a dark abyss,
Sobbing loudly, but no one can hear him.
The ship is a stranded animal.

Steven Sykes (10)
St Margaret Clitherow's Catholic Primary School, Middlesbrough

The Shipwreck

The ship is a stranded lion
Being dragged to its death,
Silently, slowly,
Crying out loud for help.
It is like a wolf crying for food,
And a stranded child.

Georgie Elcoate (10)
St Margaret Clitherow's Catholic Primary School, Middlesbrough

The Ship

The ship is a stray dog,
Abandoned and alone.
It is like a heart
Filled with misery and sadness.
Grabbing the water and gasping for life,
The ship is a broken heart hoping to live.

Megan Rutledge (10)
St Margaret Clitherow's Catholic Primary School, Middlesbrough

The Ship

The ship is a pool of sorrow,
Damp and destroyed.
It's like a crew of hopes and dreams flowing away.
The ship is like a human, swimming to survive.
The ship is a homeless animal
Trying to get a new home.

Sam Westgarth (11)
St Margaret Clitherow's Catholic Primary School, Middlesbrough

The Ship

The ship is like a dying lion needing help.
It is like a heart filled with sadness and misery.
The ship is like grabbing onto wood
And gasping for life.
The ship is a broken heart,
Hoping for life.

Luke Leka (10)
St Margaret Clitherow's Catholic Primary School, Middlesbrough

The Ship

The ship is an abandoned puppy,
Scared and scattering out in the sea.
It is like a shivering, shouting, shaking
Girl paddling from the side,
Searching for dry land.
The ship is a half-hearted animal.

Danny Jinks & Ebony Tapping (9)
St Margaret Clitherow's Catholic Primary School, Middlesbrough

The Stricken Ship

The ship is a broken heart
Pleading for help.
Battered and bruised
It is like a death trap.
Nothing to its name,
The ship is an abandoned child.

Hannah Conway (10)
St Margaret Clitherow's Catholic Primary School, Middlesbrough

The Stricken Ship

The ship is an animal stranded on an island,
Painfully pleading to be freed.
It is like a child being left alone, whimpering,
As the ship cries and wipes its eyes.
The ship is a panicking animal
Running around in circles.

Zach Greenwell (10)
St Margaret Clitherow's Catholic Primary School, Middlesbrough

The Shipwreck

The ship is a lost and lonely child,
Terrified and torn apart.
It is like a wounded heart
Bleeding to its death.
The ship is an empty soul.

Jamie Webster (9)
St Margaret Clitherow's Catholic Primary School, Middlesbrough

The Ship

The ship is a fading world,
Dripping and drowning.
Like a weeping willow,
A sinking swimmer,
The ship is a suffering animal.

Lydia Hearn (9) & Liam Elsdon (10)
St Margaret Clitherow's Catholic Primary School, Middlesbrough

The Ship

The ship is an injured animal,
Dull, destroyed and nearly dead.
It was like being in a war,
Sitting silently, sinking peacefully.
The ship is an abandoned animal.

Mollie Kane (10)
St Margaret Clitherow's Catholic Primary School, Middlesbrough

Kiss Of Death

Assassin inspirer
Sky diver
Worm snatcher
Meat catcher
Loud caller
Fast faller
Death scooper
Deadly swooper
Hole raider
Sky invader
Wind surfer
Kiss of death.

Kieran Bailey Beer (11)
St Theresa's Catholic Primary School, Sheffield

Duck

Swift flyer
Fish irritator
Cheeky sneaker
Bread eater
Naughty pincher
Loud yeller
Egg layer
Synchronised swimmer
Water prancer
Nest maker.

Heidenara Carvalho (11)
St Theresa's Catholic Primary School, Sheffield

The Terrific Parrot

Sunflower eater
Flesh biter
Human talker
Feather cleaner
House squawker
Bird protector
Feather plucker
Beak sharper
Silence breaker
Cage rattler.

Courtney Wright (11)
St Theresa's Catholic Primary School, Sheffield

Owl

Death scooper
Sky diver
Death eater
Head spinner
Nest lover
Claw digger
Night surfer
Body coverer
Jaw breaker
Gold razor.

Reece Major (10)
St Theresa's Catholic Primary School, Sheffield

Owl

Head twirler
Mouse hunter
Night catcher
Egg hatcher
Body cuddler
Owl huddler
Happy snatcher
Body catcher
Cute peeker
Little sneaker.

Courtney McClymont (11)
St Theresa's Catholic Primary School, Sheffield

Duck

Egg layer
Group swimmer
Bread stealer
Nest maker
Head ducker
Pond lover
Wing flapper
Attention seeker
Body coverer
Fly snapper.

Maisie Wilson (10)
St Theresa's Catholic Primary School, Sheffield

The Owl

Moon walker
High flyer
Sky flyer
Mouse assassinator
Night stalker
Tree hider
Stealth killer
Super hearer
Quick killer
Human haunter.

Harry Linsley (11)
St Theresa's Catholic Primary School, Sheffield

Owl

Tree peeker
Mouse catcher
Head swizzler
Night stalker
Fantastic hearer
Moon walker
Moon lover
Woodland flyer
Great seer
King of the trees!

Ashley Lane (11)
St Theresa's Catholic Primary School, Sheffield

Owl!

Night stalker
Mice catcher
Head turner
Sky flyer
Nest builder
Eye sighter
Mouse assassinator
Night walker
Food scurrier.

Olivia Walsh (11)
St Theresa's Catholic Primary School, Sheffield

Shark

Flesh eater
Blood lover
Limb loser
Fish slicer
Sneak attacker
Teeth sharpener
Human finder
Cave sleeper.

Imogen Norcliffe (10)
St Theresa's Catholic Primary School, Sheffield

River Poem

The river is a bouncy rabbit,
She's white and black.
She jumps on all the rocks all day,
Her paws get really dirty.
She licks, licks, licks.
She's deep in the river as the river sways.
She runs off the riverbank,
The stones dance all day.
She sits in the river, the same colour as her.
She likes to make chattering sounds.

April Barton (9)
The Humberston CE Primary School, Grimsby

River Poem

The river is a huge tiger,
Muscly and fierce,
He plays in the jungle all day,
With his razor blade teeth and his hairy jaws,
Hour upon hour he roars,
The gathering pebbles and the white river,
As he moans, moans, moans, moans!
The huge river tiger invades,
Licking his sharp paws.

When the night winds screech,
When the sun sleeps in the stormy clouds,
He bends down to his fierce paws,
And he roars and he claws,
Shaking his bleeding sides over the cliffs,
And he growls and howls all day long.

But on quiet days in May and June,
Whenever the grasses have dew,
Roll no more on the lovely grass,
With his head between his paws,
He runs on the grassy floors,
So quick, so quiet, he curiously explores.

Harry Seddon (9)
The Humberston CE Primary School, Grimsby

A River Poem

The river is a starving wolf,
Aggressive and grey.
He prowls down the mountain all day,
Hunting his prey.
He howls in the moonlight, loud and long.
His soft hair brushes along the bank.
Hour upon hour he hunts and gnaws,
The golden sand blowing and whistling,
And pounces, pounces, pounces, pounces.
The fast wolf growls,
Cleaning his greasy paws and fur.

And when the night wind blows,
And the glistening reflection of the moon shines,
He leaps to his feet and yawns and stretches,
Raising his head high.
He zooms his way forward,
He hollers and whimpers, strong and proud.

Megan Huntley (9)
The Humberston CE Primary School, Grimsby

A River Poem

The river is a wild cat,
Giant and grey.
He purrs beside the river all day,
With his sharp white teeth and his furry paws.
Minute upon minute, yet again he yawns.
The clashing, rumbling stones
And miaow, miaow, miaow.
The giant river-cat rolls,
Licking his greasy fur.

And when the night wind hisses,
And the moon rocks in a stormy cloud,
He jumps to his feet and plays,
Shaking his wet fur onto the ground.
He yawns and licks, long and loud.

Mollie Stansfield (10)
The Humberston CE Primary School, Grimsby

A River Poem

The river is a wet octopus,
Red and green.
He slithers down the mountain all day,
With his sucking tentacles
Sticking along the riverbank.
Hour upon hour he clings to each rock,
The sticky, slimy stones,
And, 'Fish, fish, fish, fish,'
The greedy octopus shouts,
Washing his slimy tentacles!

Joshua Capes (9)
The Humberston CE Primary School, Grimsby

The River

The river is like a playful wolf,
Huge and grey.
She sneaks down the mountain all day,
With her jagged teeth and fierce claws.
Hour upon hour she howls with the wind,
The rippling, splashing water,
And howl, howl, howl!
The beautiful river-wolf cries,
Searching for prey to eat.

And when the sunset comes
And the moon starts to appear,
She leaps to her giant paws
And howls at the moon,
Showing her enormous teeth over the rocks.

Jasmine Burnley (10)
The Humberston CE Primary School, Grimsby

The River Poem

The river is a fierce lion,
Gold and brown.
She roars as loud as she can all day.
With her long tail and her snapping teeth,
She eats her food quickly.
Hour upon hour she licks herself to keep clean.
Running really fast she crushes stones on the ground
And *roar, roar, roar, roar,* the scary lion yawns!
She jumps high, while landing without fear,
And runs to the riverbank.

Jordon-Holly Cowling (10)
The Humberston CE Primary School, Grimsby

The River Amazon

The Amazon is a huge river, giant and long.
As she stretches out her long neck
She will reach the rough sea.
She is tired and exhausted after
She has made a long and hard journey.
Her sides are rippling as she calms down and relaxes,
She gives a big, long yawn.
She gives a little march as she pulls up the pebbles
From underneath the river bed and she gives a long sigh.
The long, lazy river bangs her strong tail across the riverbank
As further downstream her river still trickles.
She swerves downhill, crashing over the bank sides,
As she moans and groans, *munch, munch, crunch, crunch.*
She soon sleeps peacefully after a big dinner.

Georgia Fleming (9)
The Humberston CE Primary School, Grimsby

The River Poem

The river is a vicious lion,
Giant and sharp.
He leaps in the forest all day,
With his razor-blade paws and his muscly body.
Hour upon hour he moans,
And he explores, explores, explores, explores.
The hunger and roars,
He whimpers as he snores.
The giant lion grumps and pounces,
Licking his long, thick legs.
The night comes, the lion rests on his little bed.
He fights in the nights,
And the moon rocks, flowing in the stormy skies.
He shakes the mud off his mane over the cliffs.

Daniel Smith (10)
The Humberston CE Primary School, Grimsby

The River

The river is a huge lion,
Furry and golden.
He crashes against the bank all day
With his assassin-blade teeth and powerful legs.
Hour upon hour he roars.
The pebbles above crash on his head.
He moans, moans, moans about it.
The giant river-lion roars,
Bounding towards the sea,
Crashing against all the rocks.

Elliot Miller (9)
The Humberston CE Primary School, Grimsby

A River Poem

The river is a humongous elephant,
He sways his long, heavy trunk,
Hitting the rippling river bed.
He charges, he pounds and *stomp, stomp, stomp,*
His thick, dark skin.
Glancing at the scorching sun,
The giant grey figure
Raises his long, winding trunk,
Blaring a deafening and thunderous sound,
The strong sound echoing around the misty mountains.

Harry Carberry (9)
The Humberston CE Primary School, Grimsby

A River Poem

The river is a greedy octopus,
Purple and blue.
He wiggles down the loud waterfall every day.
He swirls and curls through the meanders
As he slowly makes his way to the town,
With the silent screeching stones as they fall off the riverbank.
The giant river octopus moans as he shouts for food.
As the octopus gets tired, he goes calm and goes to sleep,
Then he wakes up in the sunlight in the morning.

Declan Shaw (9)
The Humberston CE Primary School, Grimsby

The River

The river is like a greedy cat,
Fluffy and soft.
She plays in the water all day, making ripples
With her silky ears and sharp claws.
Hour upon hour she resets on the bank.
The rolling, tumbling pebbles,
And purrs, purrs, purrs, purrs!
The excited river-cat yawns,
Washing her dirty paws.

Elise Milner (10)
The Humberston CE Primary School, Grimsby

A River Poem

The River Amazon is like a fierce lion,
Light brown.
He leaps over rocks all day long,
With his sleepy, long tail dangling down in the water,
And hour upon hour he roars,
With the happy, dancing rocks,
And roar, roar, roar.
The giant lion runs along the river
And then snores, snores, snores.

Alex Baker (9)
The Humberston CE Primary School, Grimsby

The River

The river is a lively elephant,
Gigantic and grey.
She stomps on the riverbank all day
With her beautiful trunk brushing along the river bed.
Hour upon hour she sits in the meander.
The hopping, leaping pebbles jump
As she stomps, and the weed, weed, weed.
The excited elephant raises her trunk
Spraying a huge jet of water in the air.

Marnie Goodfellow (9)
The Humberston CE Primary School, Grimsby

A River Poem

The river is an energetic tiger,
Giant and dangerous.
He hunts for the whole night
With his razor-sharp teeth and stealth-like stripes.
Hour upon hour he roars,
The rattling, clashing bones,
And flesh, flesh, flesh.
The giant river-tiger purrs,
Clawing his victim.

Sam Tutass (9)
The Humberston CE Primary School, Grimsby

A River Poem

The river is a golden lion,
Giant and scary.
He runs, every day he snaps.
With his sharp, vigorous claws, he runs very fast.
Hour upon hour he leaps.
The rumbling, tumbling stomach,
And scratch, scratch, scratch, scratch,
The giant lion kills,
Licking his giant paws.

William Allison (9)
The Humberston CE Primary School, Grimsby

The River Lion

The river is a fierce lion,
Grunts and growls,
He tiredly sleeps on the rocks all day,
With his shaggy jaws and evil eyes.
Day by day he stalks his prey.
The pouncing pebbles bounce along the rocks
And his eyes get wider, wider and wider.
The loud river lion roars,
Washing his tired, sweaty paws.

Sam Rice (10)
The Humberston CE Primary School, Grimsby

River Poem

The river is like a bouncing rabbit,
Black and white.
The river hops over the rocks
Like a rabbit jumping in the field.
The cracking and snapping waves,
Chatter, chatter, chatter, go the waves.
The giant river-rabbit squeaks
And it lays down licking its fluffy fur.

Jake Healey (9)
The Humberston CE Primary School, Grimsby

The River Poem

The river is a hungry horse,
Murky brown and tall.
She trots round the mountains all day,
With her winding tail she hits the muddy banks.
Hour upon hour she rests gently.
The tip-tapping pebbles dance
And the merry horse jumps.

Ellie Mumby (9)
The Humberston CE Primary School, Grimsby

Mother Nature Tenderly Laid Down

Mother Nature tenderly laid down
Blankets of ice-cold snow,
The robin that buried his dainty feet
Beneath mountains of fluffy snow.

Mother Nature tenderly laid down
Carmine berries wearing forged crowns of royalty,
The skimpy tree that waited hopefully
For the blinding sun to appear,
As a parade of snow crashed around it.

Mother Nature tenderly laid down
The touch of frost that rested on the tip of the robin's beak,
Whose watchful eye looked desperately around,
Trying to ignore his starving, aching belly,
Trying to push down the disease of worry
Going on in his tiny mind.

Mother Nature tenderly laid down
Our wonderful winter wonderland we have been given,
Asking us kindly
To take care of it.

Rachel McGlashan (11)
Walkley Primary School, Sheffield

Winter Moments

Winter moments when . . .
The frozen oak tree,
So different since it shed its golden leaves
Which lie buried under the thick blanket of snow
Which spreads up the thick trunk of the enormous oak.
It stands alone, not even a leaf to keep it company.
The huge oak stands proud like a king
In the middle of an empty meadow,
With the tips of its long, beautiful, naked branches
Touching, reaching for the icy cold sky.

Winter moments when . . .
The handsome robin
Beats the stunning snow's beauty,
With its chocolate-brown back
And the crimson feathers upon its small, soft chest.
Every little feather is detailed with delicacy.
The morning sun shines,
Showing glowing, crisp, white snow,
With the beautiful brown bird's
Small, delicate footprints engraved upon it.

A winter moment is a moment of happiness,
When dainty snowflakes
Dance down an invisible staircase.

The winter moment is a moment of freedom,
Miles of blank, empty fields.
The spring has been defeated.
It lays still . . .
Waiting . . .
Cold . . .
Lonely . . .

Ethne Smith (10)
Walkley Primary School, Sheffield

My Winter Is . . .

A scarlet-fronted robin precariously perched
On the snow-laden branch,
Waiting for the herald of spring.

A cluster of ruby berries adds a splash of colour
As they shiver and fall to the ground,
One
By
One.

A group of elderly trees gossip about winter
As the snow-coated field enviously looks on.

A queen-like oak tree, standing proudly,
Gazing over her dominion,
Silhouetted against a cloud-strewn azure sky.

A lone frond vainly lies on its throne of emerald, frosted grass,
Boasting about its lacy shawl of delicate ice.

A dawdling stream flows through snow-capped rocks and banks
To its final destination of the icy, cold lake.

A little bird house sadly waits under its blanket
Of soft, white, chilly snow, to be cleaned and filled . . .
Although birds haven't come for months.

A final crisp brown leaf resolutely clings to the brittle twig,
Determined not to fall.

This is my winter,
The winter I see,
The winter I love . . .

Nicola Purslow (10)
Walkley Primary School, Sheffield

The Cold Winter Days

The winter sun tries to brighten up
The bleak, barren hillside.
The slow stream drifts softly
Over the powerful, overlying rocks.

The oak tree casts a shadow
Across the blanket of snow.

The small but mighty robin,
Resting on a tall hill of snow,
Like a king on its throne
Watching over its chilly land.

The young robin has petite feet
Firmly planted in the ground.
The neglected bird box
Waits patiently for birds to come.

Covered in snow,
The abandoned bird house
Is surrounded by bare branches.

The last leaf,
Attached to a thread-like branch,
Determined to hang on
With all its strength.

Kayna Baugh (11)
Walkley Primary School, Sheffield

The Winter Brings . . .

The winter brings . . .
Crisp flakes of snow, precariously poised
On prickly pine needles, like tightrope walkers.

A solitary birdhouse hanging on the wall,
With a blanket of fluffy snow
Using the roof as a place to rest.

Chestnut leaves carefully balancing
Along the branch,
Trying their very best not to plunge
Onto the sharp, frosty grass.

A robin perched on a tree branch,
His fiery red chest
Brightening up the bitter, dreary winter day . . .

The pretty, ruby-red berries crying out to the birds,
'Devour me! Taste my attractiveness!'

A cold winter's day
Brings a cold winter stream trickling.
Down from the mountains
It splashes and gurgles
Past the small, startled rocks
Battling against the water.

Charlotte Rose Butler (10)
Walkley Primary School, Sheffield

Winter

The robin stood as proud
As a magnificent king
Over his precious, snow-covered land.

The sun broke out
Over the mighty hills,
As the stream trickled by.

As the red berries
Sprinkled snow like icing sugar
On each other,
The great oak stood, sturdy,
Watching and waiting.

And one little leaf
Clinging on, knowing that it will
f
a
l
l
Some day!

Arianne Zajac (11)
Walkley Primary School, Sheffield

Winter Poem

The mighty oak, proud as a king,
Watching over the cowering bushes.
Restlessly, the last resilient leaf of winter
Clings to the grand tree,
Refusing to fall.

Robin - the silent warrior - stands,
Watching the dainty worm,
Waiting for the time to strike.
As the tiny worm makes its way back home,
The warrior swoops down
And snatches it from the path.

As he flies past the empty trees,
Crimson berries lie lifelessly
On the snow-covered branches,
Waiting for winter to end.

Joe Skilbeck-Dunn (11)
Walkley Primary School, Sheffield

Winter Poem

The tiny robin has a blood-red chest
And legs like miniature twigs.

The deserted field is covered
In a strong, heavy blanket of white snow,
And the sparkling, muscular tree
Taunts the miniature snowflakes.

The leaf, covered in diamonds,
Boasts to the grass.
But they *don't* know
How sad they make her.

Joshua Higgins (10)
Walkley Primary School, Sheffield

Winter Days To Remember

The tree was king, sitting proudly
On a throne of snow.

Robin perched on the thread-like branch,
Searching for its food,
Waiting.

The river trickled down the rocks,
Slipping and sliding,
Covered with a white blanket.

The last, lonely leaf
Clung silently to the branch,
Refusing to fall.

Then that was the end . . .
The leaf fell!
Autumn was over!

Eleanor Neath (11)
Walkley Primary School, Sheffield

Winter Comes

Emerald needles like hedgehogs' spines,
Watched in admiration.
Crystals sparkled on their toes,
Soft snow resting on fragile twigs.
Crimson berries cling on to life.

A discarded leaf was a diamante dress worn by a princess.
Snow snuggled to the lonely birdhouse,
A petite robin stood submerged in snow.
The nostalgic leaf hung on,
With only the strength of the snow.

Olivia Drewery (10)
Walkley Primary School, Sheffield

Subtle Snow

Snow, snow, it's everywhere,
All on the ground, up in the air.

The snow's like a blanket,
Wrapping up the trees.
The leaves are rustling softly,
Just like a summer breeze.

Snow, snow, it's everywhere,
All on the ground, up in the air.

The snow feels so pure,
Crunching under your feet.
Although it feels so nice,
It's not as good to eat!

Snow, snow, it's everywhere,
All on the ground, up in the air.

The snow's visit has been lovely,
But sometime soon it has to end.
We all loved it lots,
But we can still pretend.

Snow, snow, was everywhere,
None on the ground, or in the air.

Emily Winfield (10)
Wheldrake with Thorganby CE (A) School, Wheldrake

Snowfall At Night

The snow falls down, guided by the light.
Night-time is upon us.
The snow glows against the darkness.
The snow glows to make everything light.

I hold the snow and ice, so clear,
The smell of pureness fills my lungs
As the snow dances on.

The snow shines at her predators
As the sun comes near,
And the little black cat
Asks why he dared to follow.

An abandoned nest catches my eye
As I crunch through the night.
The snow finally rests
And the church bells chime three.

Winter is here tonight.
Winter is here tonight.

Carla Woodcock (11)
Wheldrake with Thorganby CE (A) School, Wheldrake

The Snow

Falling softly to the ground,
Making hardly any sound,
Crunching, crackling under your feet,
Not good when it meets the heat.

So fluffy and white,
What a beautiful sight.
Powdery, sprinkly, icy and strange,
To frozen berries and abandoned nests,
Whilst tweeting birds try and rest.

Like a mode on a fan,
Falling faster than you can
Count the flakes here and there.
Oh no, they're everywhere!

Snowing, snowing all day long,
Little snowflakes growing strong.
All the children laugh and play,
They laugh, play and chat all day.

Niamh Devlin (11)
Wheldrake with Thorganby CE (A) School, Wheldrake

Snowy Days

Snowflakes falling all around
Making a crumbling sound.
The coldness melts in your mouth,
All the birds are flying south.

The snow is falling far and yonder,
How far will it fall is mine to ponder.
Each little icicle, pretty and unique,
They fall to the ground as you speak.

Woolly jumpers keep us warm,
Let's hope they don't get torn.
The fire's on, blazing hot,
Although I'd rather be hot than not!

Now this is where my poem ends,
About snow and everything that depends
On you to make up the last bit . . .
Be creative and that's it.

Rose Mitchell (10)
Wheldrake with Thorganby CE (A) School, Wheldrake

Snowflake

Snowflake, snowflake,
It lies upon the frozen lake.
It glistens in the midday sun,
When all the children are having fun.

The blanket of snow, all soft and still,
Broken by sledges gliding down the hill.
Shouts of laughter, screams of delight,
All over too soon as day turns to night.

As the sun goes down, the temperature drops,
As people rush home and all traffic stops.
It is silent and eerie, with no one in sight,
It is cold and bleak as day turns to night.

Swirling, twirling, fluttering down,
Gently covering the sleepy town,
It dances in the midnight moon,
The fluttering steps that could go on till noon.

Charlotte Exton (10)
Wheldrake with Thorganby CE (A) School, Wheldrake

Snow Has Come!

Snow is falling, winter has come,
But the only thing is . . . it makes my feet numb.
They tingle like mad,
But it doesn't make me sad
Because I love snow.
I know it can be cold,
I know it can be freezing,
I know it can be bad,
But it doesn't make me sad.
No, it doesn't.

So play in the snow and have some fun,
Now, before it melts away.
When it's all slush it goes all wet.
The white has gone,
But it will come again next year,
Well, let's bet!

Eleanor Hardy (11)
Wheldrake with Thorganby CE (A) School, Wheldrake

Snowflakes, Snowflakes

Snowflakes, snowflakes,
Falling all around,
As they land on the playground,
Children running, having fun,
Up until the day is done.

Snowflakes, snowflakes,
Tumble to the ground,
Making a pitter-patter sound.
As I tread through the snow,
Crumple, crumple, here I go.
Crumple, crumple, here I go.

Emily Pearse (11)
Wheldrake with Thorganby CE (A) School, Wheldrake

Snow, Snow, Beautiful Snow

Snow, snow, beautiful snow,
How, how it seems to glow.
A blanket of snow is upon the grass,
Which makes people smile as they pass.
Time after time it makes you cold,
Almost as pretty as solid gold,
Now snowflakes fall to the ground,
So pretty, hardly making a sound.
In the day, children have fun snowball fights,
Later on, the snow glistens in the lovely moonlight.
I hear children shouting as loud as can be,
I see icicles hung high on a tree.
But sadly the snow isn't here to stay
And very soon it will melt away.

Lucy Jones (10)
Wheldrake with Thorganby CE (A) School, Wheldrake

Through The Snow

The snow is downy from the eastern air,
Going any further, I do not dare.
It would punch and smack at my peaceful skin,
However, I know I'll never win.

Gently the ice perched itself
On a branch of a nearby conifer tree,
And the bulrushes attempting to
Break through the ice and be free.

The field looks like a blank, white piece of paper
That has been crumpled by an enraged teenager.
I am ever so sorry I must go
Through the snow, through the snow.

Sophie Heldt (11)
Wheldrake with Thorganby CE (A) School, Wheldrake

Young Writers Information

We hope you have enjoyed reading this book - and that you will continue to enjoy it in the coming years.

If you like reading and writing poetry drop us a line, or give us a call, and we'll send you a free information pack.

Alternatively if you would like to order further copies of this book or any of our other titles, then please give us a call or log onto our website at www.youngwriters.co.uk.

Young Writers Information
Remus House
Coltsfoot Drive
Peterborough
PE2 9JX
(01733) 890066